KINO GUIDE II

A Life of Eusebio Francisco Kino, S.J.
Arizona's First Pioneer
and
A Guide to His Missions and Monuments

Texts by Charles W. Polzer, S.J.
Cartography by Donald Bufkin
Historic Photo Selection by Thomas H. Naylor

Southwestern Mission Research Center
Tucson, Arizona
1982

PREFACE

When this modest book first appeared in 1968, its sole purpose was to provide for the general public a complete and up-to-date account on Padre Kino, truly one of the great figures of Southwestern history. So much had happened in the last several years, we felt it imperative to reprint a revised edition of *A Kino Guide*. Together with the additions that appeared at that time we also published a Spanish version entitled *Eusebio Kino, S. J.: Padre de la Pimería*. Although the Spanish version was soon out-of-print, the Governor of Sonora issued a new edition with a revised format in 1981. The current and expanded *Kino Guide II* has been written against a background of a decade of experience of mission tours in northern Mexico. The later story of the missions founded by Padre Kino is explained at greater length than before; in this way Kino takes his deserved place in a distinguished history of service to the native peoples of America as waves of Western ideas reshaped the New World.

None of the publications of the Southwestern Mission Research Center would have ever been possible without the generous support of sustaining members and friends. This particular edition, *Kino Guide II,* is a singular tribute to Jane Harrison Ivancovich and Helen G. Murphey of Tucson whose staunch interest in Spanish colonial history and the heritage of the greater Southwest are almost legend. When Padre Kino corresponded with the Duchess of Aveiro in the 1680's, he could have never foretold the support he would be given in the 1980's by dedicated people living in his beloved Pimería Alta.

With continuing support the publication program of the Southwestern Mission Research Center will bring several more popular and scholarly books to the general public. We believe our southwestern heritage is worth preserving and sharing. Whatever we accomplish through this program will be in direct relation to the continuing, generous support we have received through the years from members and friends of the Southwestern Mission Research Center.

Just as the Spanish version of *A Kino Guide* was a result of the hard work of Rev. José J. Romero, S. J., a long time friend and educator in Spain and of Prof. Jorge Olvera, a companion on Mexican trails and a colleague in history, so, too, is a *Kino Guide II* the product of many shared hours on the trail of truth and adventure. I would particularly like to thank Don Bufkin for his dedicated work in bringing this book into being, and I especially want to thank Thomas H. Naylor for years of patient friendship that made the quest for new knowledge rewarding and memorable.

Charles W. Polzer, S. J.
Tucson, Arizona
February, 1982

CONTENTS

EUSEBIO FRANCISCO KINO, S.J.

PIONEER PADRE OF THE PIMERÍA ALTA

The desert appears lifeless, deserted, void. Its arid mountains are etched in emptiness by the strong shadows of the parching sun. Mesas of mesquite and cactus are ripped apart by bouldered arroyos. Stillness covers the sun baked horizons. To each generation the desert seems history-less and hostile. It is no place for man, much less his dreams.

This is how the desert appears to one who has never probed its realities, for the desert is alive and filled with the dreams of men who have made history here. The desert is a paradox. It has been for centuries a home for strong men, for men of faith and vision. The desert is a place where life means more because it is set against the backdrop of nature.

This is the story of a man who knew the paradox of the desert — Eusebio Francisco Kino, priest and missionary to the Pimería Alta. He spent his life among backward desert peoples, turning river banks into farms, dirt into dwellings and churches, and dreams into living realities. He respected this land and matched its strength. Padre Kino wrote into the sands of the southwestern deserts a history as strongly etched in time as the mountains that witnessed his work.

Many men have come to the desert and made history—Cabeza de Vaca, Coronado, Oñate, Anza, and Garcés, but none have equalled the record of this dedicated Jesuit missionary. His vision reached beyond the thirsting horizon and his influence has spanned centuries, so well did he know the desert land and its people.

When Padre Kino arrived on the "Rim of Christendom" in 1687, he was already an experienced missionary although a newcomer to northern New Spain. His assignment to the frontier of the Pimería Alta, the land of the Upper Piman Indians, had been another unforeseen development in a life long series of circumstances that seemed like continued reversals. But nothing ever dampened his enthusiasm or dimmed his dreams.

The saga of Padre Kino began in Segno, a tiny mountain town in the Italian Tyrol, not far from historic Trent. There on August 10, 1645, Eusebio was born in a typical stone and timber house similar to those that stud the slopes of the Dolomite Alps along the Val di Non. His boyhood here shaped the powerful frame that would one day explore the mountains and deserts of a land a hemisphere away. Young Eusebio must have shown some degree of brilliance because his parents sent him off to the Jesuit college at Trent where he was introduced to the world of science and letters. Soon he journeyed to the Jesuit college at Hall near Innsbruck, Austria, to carry on a newly won interest in science and mathematics. While studying here, he contracted an unidentified illness that brought him close to death. That sickness drew from Kino one of his deep-down dreams — for he vowed that if his patron, St. Francis Xavier, would intercede for his health, he would enter the Society of Jesus. His health did return and for the rest of his life Eusebio Kino valued his recovery as a gift from

God through the intercession of Xavier. Whatever may be said of Kino's recovery, his life was certainly to be a welcome gift for the "abandoned souls" of Baja California and the Pimería Alta.

Now twenty years old, Eusebio Kino set foot on the long trail of Jesuit training typical of the men of the "Company of Jesus." Entering at Landsberg, he followed the intensive course of studies through Ingolstadt, Innsbruck, Munich, and Oettingen — all excellent universities in his time. Toward the end of his theological studies the Duke of Bavaria invited the young priest to teach science and mathematics at the University of Ingolstadt. Kino, however, had some years previously requested to be sent to the China mission, and as he completed his training at Oettingen, word arrived that he and a fellow Austrian were being sent. It looked as though his dreams of China were to come true. But no. One of the two was destined for the Philippines; the other, for Mexico, and Padre Kino drew the wrong slip of paper.

It was 1678 when Kino strode up the slopes of Segno to say goodbye to childhood haunts, his family, and friends. Then in mid-June he embarked from Genoa with eighteen companions, sailing for Cádiz in high hopes of catching the summer *flota* for the New World. A bit of wrong navigation in the fog and swift currents of the Straits of Gibraltar brought the packet-ship close to Ceuta; the error consumed valuable time. As they approached the Bay of Cádiz on July 13, the Imperial Spanish Fleet was already standing out to sea, bound for New Spain.

To miss the fleet was not quite like missing a transatlantic steamer. Padre Kino and companions had to wait two years to book new passage! However, the time was spent in mastering Spanish and making other useful, if remote, preparations in Seville. The Jesuit missionaries finally got places on the *Nazareno,* embarking in July, 1680. The fleet weighed anchor for Mexico, but the *Nazareno* scudded into the sand spit of the "Big Diamond" at the mouth of the Bay of Cádiz; it was promptly battered and smashed by wind and wave. Drenched, baggage-less, and dismayed, Kino waited another six months in Cádiz and got his chance in January to broach the Atlantic barrier to his destiny.

Kino's family home — Segno, Italy

Undoubtedly Kino felt much at home as he climbed the mountain trails from Veracruz to Mexico City. His Atlantic crossing had been uneventful and his arrival in Mexico, routine. There was a rumor in the wind that he might be reassigned to the Orient, or at least to the Philippines. But a new expedition to Baja California needed the skills of the neo-missionary. Admiral Isidro Atondo signed Padre Kino on as missionary and Royal Cartographer. Again, Kino had to wait while preparations for this expedition were completed in Mexico City. But Kino had learned how to use his time; he penned a small book on a recent comet. This book of medieval astronomy earned the raging rebuttal of the Mexican savant Don Carlos Sigüenza y Góngora. Wise about people and whimsical with the world's ways, Padre Kino presented the book to Don Carlos the day before he went west. Sigüenza was furious, but Kino was gone.

Baja California became Kino's first missionary territory. No Spanish expedition to the forbidding peninsula had yet succeeded, although colonization had often been attempted since the memorable days of Cortez. To Kino, California was a gigantic, unknown island — a possible haven for the exhausted crews of the Manila galleons.

The expedition built three ships on the Sinaloa River to make the crossing and maintain a supply line with the mainland. On the first venture the March winds blasted the boats against the windward shore of the Gulf, but finally Admiral Atondo tacked the tiny flotilla across the turbulent Gulf, and anchored in the welcome calm of *Bahia de La Paz.*

The curious newcomers rode at anchor for two days while royal proclamations were read to the roll of drums. Launches probed the estuaries of the bay, and finally after four days the retinue moved ashore. The Spaniards raised a rough compound between the sea and the tangled brush beyond the beach. Christian civilization was now straddling the fence, and its hopes rested tenuously on the balanced judgments of the colonists. Days passed before the Indians timidly entered the Spanish stockades; they had learned brutal lessons from the pearl fishers who preceded these ships of peace. Soon, though, glass beads and *pozole* and corn mush calmed their primordial fears.

Padre Kino's kindness reached out for these plain, destitute people whose lives knew little of clothing and less of shelter. Within weeks Kino had opened a trail across the sheer rock barrier that separated the tiny beach-head from the clusters of natives on the plateau. His days were filled with learning the coarse language that conveyed what meanings life held for these Guaicuro Indians. The good father's job was not only to befriend the Indians with the necessities of life, but to teach them the ways of civilization and even Christian doctrine. Baffled by a way to express

the Resurrection, the resourceful Kino stunned some flies, and when the Indians saw them "return to life," they uttered the words that then became a part of the Creed in their native tongue. Unfortunately, however, Kino did not realize the Indians had only given him the words for "they are dead." His method for stunning flies was more fascinating than the difficult doctrine he was trying to teach!

Not uncharacteristically, Baja California was unkind to the colonists. Violent storms kept Atondo's relief ships from landing supplies. Stocks dwindled and fear of starvation crept into the Spanish camp. As the summer temperatures rose, water supplies fell; food supplies shortened, and so did tempers. The fear-ridden finale to the expedition sounded when the Spanish soldiers invited some Indians, who were suspected of stealing, to a meal of peace. Suddenly into the midst of the defenseless party the Spaniards fired a round of cannon shot.

This puny act of cowardice earned the awesome threat of revenge. What had been simple Spanish fear turned into human terror. With their backs against the sea, the colonists awaited annihilation from arrows fired in justifiable anger. But the fortunate arrival of the relief ship saved them from death by starvation and snatched them from inevitable slaughter.

Padre Kino was disgusted with the soldiers' deceitful conduct and the colonists' terror-stricken decision to abandon La Paz. Only out of necessity did he join the retreat from the peninsula. The expedition regrouped on the mainland and in the fall planned a new attempt. Kino made it clear to Admiral Atondo that there should be no more fiascos resulting from the cowardly actions of soldiers or colonists. This time a new start was made at San Bruno, on the coast to the north of present day Loreto.

From this new mission station the first expeditions inched across the rocky Giantess Mountains; within four months Padre Kino had reached the shores of the South Sea, the Pacific. Friends were made among the Indians; languages were noted and learned. Baptisms were administered to infants and to the dying. After a year's effort it looked like a permanent mission had been settled in Baja California.

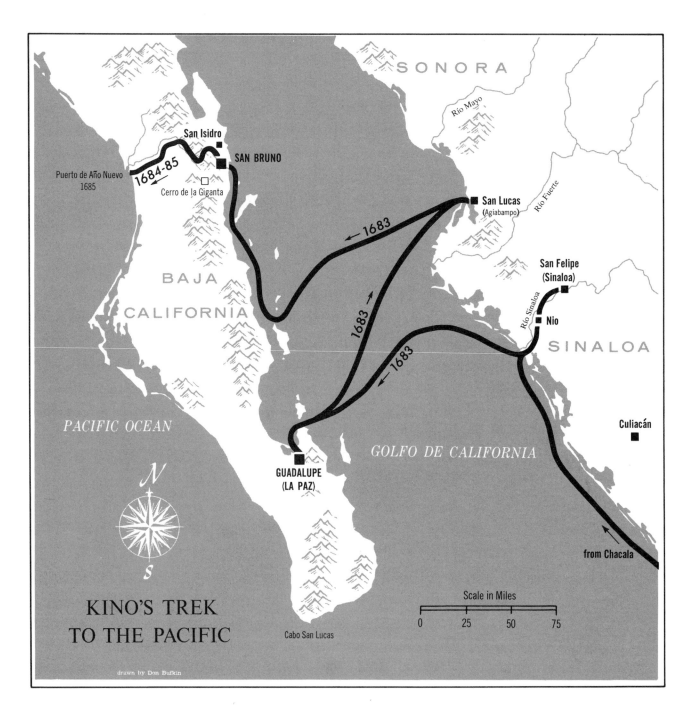

KINO'S TREK
TO THE PACIFIC

drawn by Don Bufkin

But at San Bruno the sun burned away the water, and with the water, the crops; disease swept through the settlement. The great dreams of Governor Atondo were drying up in the dust. Atondo called for a vote to abandon the royally financed California enterprise. Padre Kino dissented, but to no avail. Orders were issued to salvage as much as could be returned on the overworked ships. Then, warm winds pushed the crafts away from the coast, and Kino's own hopes dimmed as the mountains of destiny sank into the horizon. Baja California would never again

feel the tread of his boots on her wilderness trails or witness the glint of the sun on his astrolabe as he charted the secrets of the austere, rugged land.

For one fleeting moment Padre Kino felt there would be a return to California when Admiral Atondo was ordered to maintain the new conversions by the Viceroy, Conde de Paredes. The small ships were again outfitted at the harbor of Matanchel, but an urgent dispatch came from Mexico that five Dutch pirate ships were preparing to waylay the Manila galleon. Admiral Atondo dutifully intercepted the richly laden galleon and escorted it to safety at Acapulco. Padre Kino forever revelled in their successful evasion of the Dutch threat.

Once again on the mainland, Kino traveled, argued, and cajoled to regain a foothold in California, but the Audiencia at Guadalajara said the Spanish Crown wanted no part of the place — from Cabo San Lucas far north to Monterey. Padre Kino rode to Mexico City and pleaded his case for weeks. Finally the Viceroy granted him the authority to return and re-establish the missions he knew would succeed. It looked as though fortune was taking a turn. A pack train clopped into Mexico City laden with the silver that could purchase the island's future, but before it was unloaded, the Royal treasury sequestered the $80,000 to pay the French an overdue maritime indemnity. California was through — all because some impetuous Spaniard had sunk a ship in a distant European bay.

The Orient was out. California was closed. Kino was a missionary without a mission. He then suggested to his Provincial in Mexico that he be sent to work among the Seris and Guaymas tribes, who were at least close to California. He still held a glimmer of hope for Baja California. The Viceroy acceded to the Provincial's proposal and the "Padre on Horseback" trotted out of Mexico's capital a hardened, wiser man. He knew the Indian and his ways; he knew the Spaniard; he knew the Crown; he knew his Church; and he had a mission.

Warned by other Jesuit missionaries about slavery in the mines, Kino stopped at Guadalajara to discuss the situation with the Royal Audiencia. The colonials were impeding the conversion of the Indians by their forced labor policies under the *repartimiento* system. Padre Kino presented the matter to the audiencia president, Zeballos. The Audiencia swiftly communicated to Padre Kino a Royal *cédula* recently issued by Carlos II granting the Indians temporary immunity from exploitation. So when Padre Kino rode into the mountain headquarters of the Jesuit missions in Oposura, he clutched a royal decree that read like an emancipation proclamation for the Indians throughout colonial New Spain. It demanded that the Indian converts be free for twenty years from compulsory labor in the Spanish mines; it was a mandate for freedom and a guarantee of eventual education for the outclassed aborigines. This decree would become a sign of division in the battle for Christian civilization on the frontier.

Padre Kino fully expected to receive an assignment to work among the Seris and Guaymas nations; they were, in fact, the tribes closest to California. At least he could wait at the gates for the next time opportunity knocked. What Eusebio didn't know was that a decision had been made in October, 1686, that the next missionary assigned to the northern missions would be sent among the Pimas Altas. Fears of hostility had gripped the northern missions, and a Piman peace appeared crucial. Only four years had elapsed since Kino had come to the New World, but his reputation had grown enormously. Even Padre Manuel González, the Visitor of the northwestern missions, had heard of this Italian Jesuit, recognizing in him a unique talent. Perhaps the new mission among the Pimas Altas might just be suited to Kino's spirit. Certainly the uncharted deserts would challenge the scientist, and the scattered villages, the organizer.

When Kino arrived at Oposura, modern-day Moctezuma, the Father Visitor had been discussing developments on the frontier with Padre José de Aguilar, the missionary from Cucurpe. And while Kino may have hoped to receive a coastal assignment, he was beginning to learn how to keep step with the changing pace of Providence.

Together the three Blackrobes threaded their way out of the rugged *cordillera* into the Valley of the Sonora toward the perimeter of civilization. And so it happened that in the ruddy dusk of March 13, 1687, Padre Eusebio Francisco Kino cantered into Cucurpe—and history.

Cucurpe, the place "where the dove sings," nestles over the still valley of the San Miguel. It was then an outpost of empire on the rim of Christendom. For a century the Spaniards on the coast had preferred the nearby Sonora River as a convenient route to New Mexico, so there had been little purpose to penetrate the ridges toward the west. Even thought in the valleys seemed to be polarized in terms of north and south. When Kino rode out of Cucurpe the morning after his arrival, he was literally breaching the rim of Christendom and opening the minds of people to the unknown west, to the deserts and mountain barriers of the Colorado, and to California. He entered this frontier as a peacemaker to safeguard the province of Sonora; he would emerge not only as a peacemaker, but as pathfinder and pioneer as well.

The first circuit of the new mission territory was gratifying. The terrain promised rich agricultural rewards, and the Pimas were really peaceful and anxious to have their own Padre. Like so many matters in colonial New Spain, the recent conspiracy of the Pima Chief *Canito* which seemed to threaten the Sonora settlements was exaggerated and generalized. Padre Kino found less to worry him about Indian uprisings than in raising up the Indians to a better life.

The Jesuit practice in mission expansion was a carefully devised program. New missions were established only among the more permanent native settlements. The initial foundation was kept reasonably close to already functioning missions for physical and moral support. Padre Eusebio followed that practice by locating his home base, *Nuestra Señora de los Dolores,* at Cosari, only

A Pima Indian

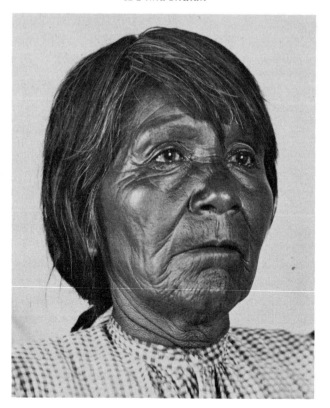

slightly higher up the shallow mountain valley from Cucurpe. His new site would be close, but quite independent. And Cosari was an ideal spot because his church and compound dominated two valleys separated by a narrow defile that closed down on the clear waters of the Río San Miguel. Dolores, Our Lady of Sorrows, may seem an unlikely patroness for such a bountiful village. Kino chose the title because he carried a fine painting of her by Juan Correa, a gift from the famous Mexican artist for his new mission.

The enthusiasm of Padre Kino became the catalyst for a new desert economy! The Pimans had farmed their lands for many generations, but never did they achieve so much as under their new missionary. Drowsy deltas sprang into productive gardens. River lands were cleared for wheat, corn and squash; slopes were readied for grapes and imported European fruit trees. Each village erected an adobe chapel and started the long-term work on the churches which would be the pride of their pueblos. And the names that Kino bestowed on the new towns have become bywords in Southwestern history — San Ignacio, Magdalena, San Xavier del Bac, Cocóspera, Caborca, Tumacácori, and Tucsón. Some names Christian, some names Indian, but all recorded in time through the industry of their founder and provider.

The hard years were the early years. Kino's presence was not appreciated by the colonial miners along the Bacanuche and the San Miguel, nor did the *hechiceros,* medicine men, take kindly to the threat to their tribal power and superstitious practices. But a program of patience with the natives and firm forthrightness with the Spaniards smashed the opposition to change and Christianization. Help arrived hard on the heels of Padre Eusebio's requests, but the incredibly harsh living conditions and slow progress among some of the Indians discouraged the new men. Kino kept on although the transfer of his new companions tried his eternal optimism.

The little chain of missions on Padre Kino's seventy-five mile circuit was mushrooming. Padre González remarked that he had never seen such growth in such a short time. And then the inevitable, grim reports — rooted in jealousy — began to circulate about the "ambitious Padre

Kino" and the "quarrelsome Indians in his charge." Both civil and religious superiors across the multiple mountain barriers became wary of this new man on their frontier. Although such reports were endemic to Spanish colonial life, they had to be investigated. So in the spring of 1690 Padre Juan María Salvatierra, the future giant of Lower California, rode into Sonora from his mission station in Chínipas with the powers of a Visitor General. His sole intent was to review the situation on the "rim" and shut the missions down if conditions even approached the rumors rampant in the interior. It was a case of Providence bringing Kino to the brink of disaster all over again.

Juan María Salvatierra

Lesser men would have crumbled under the hardships and the criticism. But Kino, true to form, met the Padre Visitador with real warmth and genuine enthusiasm. Together Kino and Salvatierra rode the hundreds of leagues linking the mission *visitas*. The land was alive with crops; villagers greeted the Blackrobes by erecting crosses and flowered arches. Indians trudged in from distant pueblos to beg Baptism for themselves and their families. Every hour of travel saw a panorama of plenty, and every hour of rest received pleas for the Faith and a missionary.

League by league the long face of Salvatierra shortened; the presumed harshness of his task was mellowed by what he saw. Finally a smile broke beneath his hawked features as enthusiasm

rose with the prospects of Christianizing this happy land. And Salvatierra heard as much as he saw, for Kino talked of the island of California and the imminent conversion of her peoples. He even suggested the construction of a boat to ply across the Gulf. Why not? The riches of Sonora could supply the wants of California!

By the time Salvatierra was ready to continue south through the extensive Jesuit missions along the Yaqui and Mayo rivers, he had learned to share the deep vision of Padre Kino. The profound conviction imparted by the Apostle to the Pimas not only staved off the foreclosure of the Sonora mission effort, but it also decided Salvatierra on courageously regaining the Californias. A whole new dimension had dawned in the Pimería. Padre Eusebio, remembering the extreme need of the peninsular people, pressed efforts to make his missions even more productive. Success in Sonora meant life for the Church in California. No one knew better than Kino and Salvatierra that without cooperation and mutual sacrifice any missionary venture is untenable and doomed to sterility.

Kino's mission district had hardly any boundaries except to the south and east. His visitas extended 200 miles north and almost as far to the west. Now the disparate system would have to be consolidated into a working unit to supply the frontier and to assist the push toward California. Westward explorations would have to be made to discover a suitable port to ship cattle to the California island.

The expansion of the Pimería was not purely a matter of founding more missions or enlarging the existing villages. The whole chain of missions under Kino's care bordered on the home country of the Apaches and their fierce, nomadic cousins, the Jocomes. A primary task was to knit a bickering Piman group, the Sobaípuris, into a firm, defensive coalition against Apache incursions. Padre Kino mounted once again and rode north from Dolores spreading the word of God and joining the tribes in peace up and down the San Pedro drainage. It was 1692; Kino was bringing to the ravaged land something it had known little of — peace and security. With each day's journey more Indian settlements were drawn into the defensive wall. Communities that had been victimized for generations found a new strength in the strange Blackrobe.

The whole northeastern frontier began to shape up under the leadership of Padre Kino and his allied chieftains. This meant that the Padre could now turn his gaze westward to penetrate the mysterious lands that lay between him and California.

Late in 1693, Padre Kino assembled a pack train to explore the lower Altar river country. The trek brought them as far west as *El Nazareno,* a high peak on the edge of the sand desert. Through the haze they saw the peaks of distant California and the arching coastline of the Gulf. California was close enough to reach by boat!

Where would he get a boat? Build one. In the desert? Certainly. The vision of Kino was a case of madness to his superiors. But the good father's orders went out for cottonwood, mesquite, and pine timbers. Pack trains wound through the passes to deposit their wooden treasures at Caborca, only one hundred and sixty kilometers west in the desert! Sheer madness—except for madness—except for confident Padre Eusebio.

It was during these first thrusts westward that Padre Eusebio's unforgettable and indefatigable trail companion arrived, Lieutenant Juan Mateo Manje. He was detached from his uncle's "Flying Company" to keep pace with Kino's advance. His presence was always good for a laugh or two as when he crashed to the ground in a cottonwood tree which he and the Indians were cutting for the keel of a boat. After that Manje stalked the desert searching for a dry route.

Although Padre Kino had orders to build his boat from the Provincial, the more proximate and sedentary Father Visitor, Juan Muñoz de Burgos, ordered the project suspended. That was agreeable enough; the wood had to season anyway. So attention was turned to the north, to rumors about a river west and a great house on its banks. It was already Advent in 1694 when Padre Eusebio visited and described Casa Grande on the Río Gila for the first time. He was beginning to realize how vast a land was opening up for Christianization.

Meanwhile, organization was catching up with all the dashing to and fro on the frontier. The missions of the Pimería Alta were grouped into a mission rectorate, Nuestra Señora de los Dolores, under their first superior, Padre Marcos Antonio Kappus, at Cucurpe. Padre Muñoz,

The slopes of El Nazareno

still in authority, clopped about reassigning missionaries. A new man had just arrived, Padre Francisco Xavier Saeta, a zealous young Jesuit from Sicily. Muñoz ordered him to the pueblo of Caborca, Kino's landlocked seaport, and Kino himself was ordered to furnish everything the new mission might need. Nothing could have pleased Kino more, although he must have smiled at the supercilious trappings of the official orders. One hundred head of cattle and one hundred and fifteen sheep and goats thundered down the Magdalena and Altar rivers to Caborca.

Then, ominously, there came another of the recurrent reversals of Providence — this time steeped in blood and racked with violence. Fired by superstitious misinterpretations of mission policy, the settlement at Tubutama erupted in revolt. The baptism of infants and the aged appeared to the faithless and resentful hechiceros as an ominous evil. They looked upon the ritual and rigid discipline as undermining their power; certainly they were being hindered from their accustomed excesses. Indian malcontents set the ripening fields on fire, wrecked the buildings, and ravaged pueblos all along the Altar river. And far downstream they murdered the wary, but defenseless Padre Saeta. In a postscript to his last letter to Kino (written the night before Saeta's martyrdom) he asked that Kino "not lose sight of him." Unfortunately the attack on Caborca came so suddenly that neither warning nor assistance was possible. Saeta's was the first martyr's blood to flow in the Pimería.

Genuine terror clutched the territory. Rumors flashed of mass attacks on the northeastern perimeter — the Jocomes, Janos, and Apaches. The entire Pimería was tensed for a fight to the death. Soldiers of General Domingo Jironza's Flying Company, the fast and far-ranging Spanish cavalry, converged on the Pimería from Fronteras and Real de San Juan. Military justice would triumph.

The Spaniards were split on how to achieve pacification. Some clamored for revenge, others suggested patience and careful condemnation of the instigators of the rebellion. On the cool morning of June 9, 1695, at the request of Padre Kino, the Pima chiefs met the awesome assembly of Spanish troops near El Tupo. It was agreed:

Indian rebellion at Tubutama, 1751

the guilty were to be handed over for proper punishment. The ringleaders of the revolt sat among the tribal chiefs and a few friendly Indians on the moist soil of La Ciénega. Encircled by mounted cavalry, the Indians confessed their regrets for the revolt. Then one spokesman dragged a guilty rebel to his feet.

The sword of Captain Antonio Solís flashed in the morning sun; a head tumbled among the astonished Indians.

Such sudden and sickening "justice" horrified the unarmed natives. This was no trial. It was a trap. Crazed with fear they bolted for the open desert and freedom. The morning air sputtered with musket fire. Justice was speaking with leaden balls and swishing swords. The innocent and loyal lay slaughtered with the handful of the guilty. And the verdict of that summer morning still hangs over that desolate spot — at a place called *"La Matanza,"* the slaughter.

Padre Eusebio Kino was utterly sick at heart. Justice was made a mockery; peace, a nearly impossible dream. Then the frontier exploded into open war for three terror-filled months. The ponderous Spanish cavalry struck fear into the Indians, but their warriors continued to dart from mountain strongholds to burn missions and fields, escaping long before the Spaniards could react. The "hawks" who put their trust in power made no progress toward peace. Frustrated and irritated by their failure, they handed

The Padre on Horseback

the problem over to Kino whose friends their justice had murdered. And typically, Padre Eusebio accepted the responsibility of bringing peace back to the Pimería. A few days and many reassurances later, peace returned. One priest did in days what confounded the agents of the Crown for months.

One might expect that after the Pimería had calmed down that Padre Kino would relax somewhat himself. But no. In November, only three months after the peace was effected, Kino was in the saddle. This time his destination was Mexico City! The 1200 mile ride was completed in seven weeks. His visit was by no means to renew old acquaintances; he rode on urgent business — to press for the reopening of the California missions and to explain what was really happening on the frontier.

Part of the Padre's explanation was made through the pages of a small book he wrote about the martyrdom of Saeta. His untimely and tragic death provided an occasion for Kino to clarify the situation in the Pimería and to elaborate on his mission methods. Kino knew he was fighting for his own missionary life; rumors had ensnared both the man and his work. So he unleashed all the talent he had in writing and drawing maps.

He really did not need to demonstrate his literary prowess, however, since Kino's plight had come to the attention of the Jesuit General Tirso González in Rome. Comparing Kino to St. Francis Xavier, the powerful head of the order made it scathingly clear to the superiors in New Spain that Kino was not to be hindered in his extraordinary efforts in the Pimería.

Padre Kino had lost none of his ability to argue a good case. The Provincial agreed to send five new men to the Pimería so the expansion could continue apace. Having spent exactly one month in Mexico City, the Padre was back in the saddle and headed homeward. From his own memoirs we learn that despite all the seeming misfortunes and setbacks dealt him by Providence, Kino was being favored all the while. The very military escort he traveled with through the ravaged Jocome terrain was ambushed and wiped out to a man; that is, all except Padre Kino who had made a brief detour to greet two old Jesuit companions!

The whole of the Pimería surged to life when Padre Eusebio returned. Chiefs of distant tribes walked scores and hundreds of miles to celebrate with him at Dolores. The Indian residents of Cosari and their visitors joined together to harvest the crops in the fertile valleys. Many who had earlier been instructed were baptized. In a way it was a miniature demonstration of what Kino's original coming to the Pimería had meant. Here were unity, friendship, industry, gaiety, and plenty revolving around a common sacramental life in the mission pueblo.

However, the years immediately following the Pima uprising of 1695 were turbulent ones for Padre Kino. The missions had to be rebuilt, confidence restored, and factions abolished. The policies of the pastor of Dolores were not too popular with some of the other missionaries in the region. Pens flared in accusation, and faces blushed with embarrassment and shock. Kino was simply not the unthinking "dead stick" he should have been, in the idealistic and unreal minds of some of his companions. "His fame was too great" — especially among the Indians. That would really never do if the man were to be a humble religious. Nothing, however, really fazed Padre Kino. He dealt as bluntly with his accusers as he did forthrightly in behalf of his Indian dependents. The Pimería was shaping up just as rapidly as before.

While Kino's critics fussed and fumed, he tirelessly drove herds of cattle and sheep into the San Pedro and Santa Cruz valleys in preparation for a whole new string of missions. Four separate *entradas* averaged nearly 200 miles each. No one could doubt that Kino was serious about a permanent shift of the mission frontier to the north. And at fifty-two years of age, his inexhaustible vigor peeved some of his confreres — particularly the younger men.

In May of 1697 the hard-riding Padre was scarcely out of the saddle when a dispatch reached Dolores from Padre Palacios, the Mexican Provincial: Kino was reassigned to California! The Crown had accepted the Kino-Salvatierra proposal to christianize California exclusive of any royal assistance. The new missionaries even held the unusual power to control military units sent to protect the missions. It was the answer to a dream.

But one man's dream is another man's nightmare. What would become of the Pimería without Padre Eusebio? The news of the transfer was one of good riddance to Padre Francisco Mora, Kino's immediate superior at Arispe; it was unthinkable to Padre Horacio Polici, the Visitor at Oposura; it appeared catastrophic to General Jironza at San Juan and the governor at Parral. Frantic letters from the north blew into Mexico City in a storm of protest. Pity the poor Provincial! One month Kino is damned by Dame Rumor and the next, deified by civil magistrates.

And what about Kino? He knew he was being stretched on the rack of obedience — with his feet in the Pimería and his head in California. While the irascible tug-of-war over his destiny was taking place, Kino calmly wrote Father General Tirso González asking to spend six months in each place. He would rather divide his time than his torso. But one thing even Kino had to admit — somehow the colonials had come to appreciate the incalculable influence of this pioneer Padre. They may have obstructed him in earlier days, but now they needed his presence.

Padre Mora, the old scrooge of the Sonora valley, scoffed that Kino had contrived the whole, mass protest! The juice from Mora's own sour-grapes mentality penned the best refutation ever to the opposition to Padre Kino.

While couriers on horseback raced the wheels of fate, Kino complied with his orders and left Dolores, the mission he founded ten years before. He rode down the San Miguel and across the scorching flatland toward the Río Yaqui. There

he would meet Padre Salvatierra and begin all over again. The desert can be a lonely place, particularly when one has just been turned out of the land to which have been given years of one's life. Padre Eusebio wasn't sad, though; in fact, he wasn't even looking back. Perhaps he should have been — because a courier galloped after him wreathed in swirling dust. Finally overtaking the Padre, the messenger displayed new and special orders from the Provincial in Mexico. Kino was to return to the Pimería, as the Viceroy himself had ordered, because the government and the people needed him!

In the life of Padre Eusebio Francisco Kino this was the moment of final fulfillment. There would be no more reversals because the pattern of his work was set. He was destined to be poised between two worlds. His new orders committed him to the Pimería but only on the assumption that Sonora and Arizona would be a base of operations. His missions had to be forged into an agricultural empire that would sustain the bleakest of California years. Now his explorations would have to seek out new ports on the Gulf. His own life would be spent more in the saddle than the sanctuary.

Mountains rise highest where valleys course deepest. The loss of Kino to the Pimería had cut a chasm into the hopes of the Indians, but his announced return propelled them back to newer heights. Warriors and chieftains, women and children converged on the good Padre of Dolores. Now they felt confident in pressing their requests since the loyal champion of their cause had come back. Kino sensed the tempo and channeled all energies into a giant pilgrimage to Bazeraca, to the feet of the Father Visitor.

Some Indians had traveled well over 200 miles to join in the welcome. Why not transform their hopes into a pilgrimage of petition? The triumphant and confident column tramped right through Arispe where Padre Mora could witness the growing popularity of his "problem" Padre. Through canyons and over rugged mountain passes the pilgrims went — through Oposura, Guásavas, right to Padre Horacio Polici. The peace march won its point: more missionaries were promised, and soldiers, too, for a new garrison at Quíburi.

The expedition which left Dolores on November 2, 1697, open a new era for the Pimería. Many expeditions had wound out of the hills near Dolores, but a new purpose was being woven into the fabric of Pima life, the sustenance of California by land and sea. Padre Kino, Manje, and ten Indians led a well-provisioned pack train northeast past Remedios, Cocóspera, and Suamca. They threaded the Huachuca Mountains and finally camped at Santa Cruz de Gaybanipitea. Close on their trail came Captain Cristóbal Bernal and twenty-two dragoons from Fronteras. The combined groups rode into Quíburi and greeted Chief Coro of the Sobaípuris who were in the midst of celebrating a victory over their hostile neighbors, the Jocomes and Janos. Seeing scalps and hearing the tales of combat, the Spaniards who had been skeptical of Sobaípuri valor joined in the wild festivities and merriment. It's always a cause for joy when one's allies are strong and effective.

From Quíburi the men of the Cross and the Crown, accompanied now by Coro and thirty braves, continued down the San Pedro valley. The column's route knifed between friend and foe because the eastern slope of the river was Apache country. Apparently the sting of defeat was still too strong, however, for they encountered only friends. The expedition reached the junction of the San Pedro and Gila and turned westward to search out the large ruins in the sprawling desert. The fascination of the great mystery surrounding the disappearance of the ancient tribes who built the great houses and aqueducts along the Gila bit deeply into the Spanish adventurers. It was eerie to be so alone where there had once been such a vast human occupation.

Padre Kino pushed on as far as San Andrés, the old Tudacsón, near modern Sacatón. Indians stained with red pigment stirred Manje's curiosity because a young warrior described the paint in a way that spelled quicksilver. What a boon a new mercury mine would mean to the silver industry of the north! With their interests slaked by new discoveries, the expedition reluctantly turned back toward the Santa Cruz river trail and home. Everyone was elated with the success of the entrada: Kino saw a new peace being born

Casa Grande before 1903

of Sobaípuri strength; Manje felt it was a step toward the reduction of the nations of North America; and the Indians were thrilled by the hearty interest shown in them by the wonderful white men from the south.

Padre Kino's plan worked. The Apaches were contained by the Pimería's solid wall of defense. Now both missionaries and military men could turn their backs on the eastern frontier. The *"tierra incógnita"* to the west spread before them in all its baffling expanse and hazy rumor. Far-ranging hunters spoke of distant people, giant rivers, and even armored white men riding antlered animals. Padre Eusebio's home mission of Dolores had suddenly ceased to be the heart of the Pimería because his mission borders were hurtling westward. Pimas, Pápagos, Sobas, Cocomaricopas, Opas, and Yumas — all the tribes of the desert west would grow accustomed to the dust clouds of Padre Kino's pack trains. He was a restless man of peace, pushing a four hundred mile frontier farther into the unknown.

It was the fall of 1698 before another major expedition was mounted. The earlier months of the year had seen the tragic plundering of Cocóspora by the Apaches, the swift and savage retaliation captained by Coro, and a resumption of boat-building at Caborca. By September Padre Kino, although still weak and tired from various illnesses, took a new captain, Diego Carrasco, and seven faithful Indians on a reconnaissance of the "great river," the Gila. He fully intended to scale the Sierra Estrella but fever cut him down and he languished for some days at San Andrés. His intentions were also to survey the Gulf Coast from the Estrellas, but the natives explained to him that the Gila flowed around these mountains and emptied into the Gulf far to the southwest!

Partially recuperated but stunned by the news about the course of the Gila, Padre Kino and Carrasco wheeled the pack train southward and cut across the heart of Papaguería. Listening to the Indian reports, they knew the trail to the Gulf would be treacherous, but they were determined to accomplish the purpose of the entrada. The Indians at Sonoita directed the explorers toward Pinacate Peak. Kino climbed its volcanic ridges to see the Gulf coast arching away to the west at today's Adair Bay. He had been wrong about the northern limits of the Gulf waters, and the Gila emptied into another great river somewhere to the north and west. From Pinacate, or Santa Clara as it was then called, they turned back and took the short route home through Caborca where fresh supplies and mounts awaited them.

The pace of the trip was typical for Kino. He had traveled some eight hundred miles in slightly more than three weeks. During the trip he took time out to baptize nearly 400 infants, instruct others in the faith, and acquaint himself with hundreds of destitute Pápagos throughout the arid land.

After a three month rest at Dolores Padre Eusebio enlisted the aid of Padre Adam Gilg and Captain Manje on a new entrada into the Papaguería. There was nothing scanty about this expedition: he assembled ninety pack animals, eighty horses, thirty-six head of cattle, eight loads of provisions, and a host of Indian vaqueros! Whatever lay to the west, Sonoita was certainly a key and he meant to establish a new mission ranch there to be a base camp for the northwest explorations. The massive column picked up even more supplies from faithful Padre Agustín de Campos at San Ignacio and moved around the hills into the Altar valley. They cut a little westward at the southern flanks of the Baboquívari Mountains and camped near the weird peak that dominates the range and the desert vistas. In nine days, on the 16th of February, 1699, they reached Sonoíta and prepared for the death-defying crossing of the *Camino del Diablo.*

The Devil's Highway is one of those ancient trails that even modern man has not reopened. Its route lies along a jagged, parched path from water tank to water hole. The thrust into the desert missed the first promised water; it was almost as if the devil himself were welcoming the explorers. They rode into the night and finally reached a granite tank glistening in the moonlight. Kino and Manje called it Moon Tank, in memory of their midnight discovery. Surrounded by desolate hills and dry plains they scurried from *aguaje* to *aguaje* — Tinajas Altas to Dripping Springs. In four days of hard riding they covered more than 125 miles and finally arrived at the "Río Grande," the Gila.

The morning after arriving at the Gila a hundred Yumans padded up the river trail to offer the newcomers gifts and words of welcome. Manje was anxious to go downriver, but Kino sensed it would be better to postpone further penetration. There was something astonishing about Kino's sensitivities to Indian protocol. But Manje managed to satisfy his curiosity by riding to a peak in the Gila mountain range from which he saw the junction of the two great rivers, the Gila and the Colorado. No more could the Gila be misnamed the "Río Grande," because the mighty Colorado made the Gila look like a creek. Following the suggestion of Padre Gilg, the Gila was renamed the *"Río de los Apóstoles,"* and when the trio left the village-camp of San Pedro, the Indian villages along the river were named in a litany of the other apostles. Reaching the great bend of the Gila they struck across the desert and negotiated a pass in the Sierra Estrella which deposited them near the familiar village of San Andrés de Coata. What a marvel Padre Kino must have been to the Pimas who watched this man in his mid-fifties pop out of the desert every few months coming almost always from a different direction!

Once again at Dolores the word traveled throughout the province that Padre Kino was back from lands of fabled riches. A whole summer was spent in crossing epistolary swords over the worth of vast desert lands accruing to Spain from Kino's explorations. Cynical colonists couldn't see the potential of the land or the people northwest of Pimería; Kino was making insects look like elephants and "painting grandeurs in Pima Land which did not exist there."

During the last week of October, 1699, Padre Antonio Leal, the new Visitor, and Padre Francisco Gonzalvo, accompanied Kino and Manje on a new entrada scheduled this time to reach the juncture of the Gila and the Colorado. Some of Padre Leal's attendants fell ill at Bac and the military escort under Cristóbal Bernal was diverted in an action with Chief Coro against the troublesome Jocomes. With the impatience of seasoned adventurers Kino and Manje dashed from village to village hoping that prospects would improve, but they didn't. Although Kino never openly remarks about his suspicions of danger along the Colorado, without an escort he could only abort the expedition and take Leal through the central Papaguería instead. The desert seemed to spring to life for the Padre Visitor since hundreds of Indians poured into each pueblo along the route. It may have been a disappointment not to have attempted the trek to the Yumans, but it was a welcome reward to see that Padre Kino was correct in his assessment of the Pima and Pápago nations.

While Padres Leal and Gonzalvo jostled wearily along the desert trails, Padre Eusebio and Captain Juan Mateo were undertaking a kind of "flying mission." In the five days they were separated from the main cavalcade, the pair rode over three hundred miles throughout the territory adjoining the main trail. Kino preached and baptized; Manje counted heads for the Crown. Apparently the main body moved faster than they anticipated, because the last day and night out Kino and Manje churned through fifty leagues of desert wash and *cholla* forest! They caught Leal and Gonzalvo at Búsanic, slept four hours, and then rose early to butcher some livestock, distribute presents and hold a civil ceremony to appoint justices. No wonder Leal and Gonzalvo were glad to get back to Dolores and rest.

But Kino wasn't in the mood to rest. Something had been bothering him since the trip to the lower Gila. The sturdy Yumans had given him a simple, precious gift — some blue abalone shells. At the time he smiled and thanked the natives, but perforce he had to concentrate on his explorations and survival. It was on the return ride when Padre Kino was reminiscing beneath the winter sun that the salty breeze and crashing surf of Baja California thundered into his memory. Those shells were seen by him only once, fifteen years before on the mapping expedition to the "opposite shore" of the Isla de California! Could there be a connection? Possibly, but not probably.

Padre Kino welcomed the turn of the century at Dolores. His work load was heavy and the new California missions under Salvatierra needed much assistance. The thrust to the Colorado just meant more work. Dolores was a long way from the new concerns on the Gila and the Colorado. It would be a prudent plan to build a mission closer to these new fields of labor, so Padre Kino chose the fertile and extensive ranchería of Bac to become the base of future northwestern entradas. The foundations of a large church were laid in 1700, but the shortage of missionaries prevented the transfer of Kino's headquarters to this favorable site.

No new blood was being pumped into the Pimería these days. Life was getting to be a bit more routine. That is, until March. A chieftain from the Gila Pimas greeted Padre Eusebio at Remedios with news of the river peoples and a gift of a cross strung with twenty blue shells from the governor of the Cocomaricopas. The cross was accepted with graciousness but once again the shells made the Padre uneasy. The unanswered question of their origin nagged at his scientific nature.

His blue-shell problem simmered for a few weeks, and then began to plague him for an answer. With ten Indian friends he set out for the Gila pueblos in late April. Enroute down the Santa Cruz he got news of possible trouble in the Soba country. He had not forgotten the tragic lessons of '95, so he pulled up short and stayed at San Xavier del Bac. He could not prudently leave the Pimería if trouble were brewing, but he could still study the problem of the blue shells by calling a conference. Runners went north,

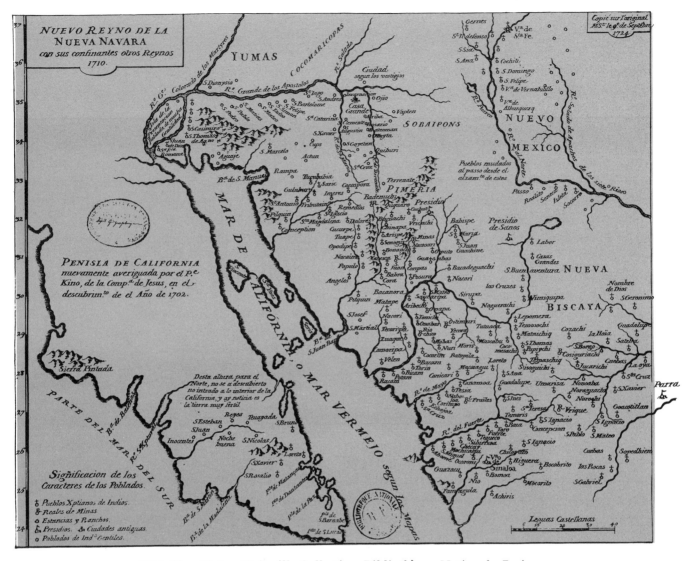

1710 Kino Map — D'Anville Collection, Bibliothèque Nationale, Paris

west and even east to call the great chiefs to the "Blue Shell Conference" at Bac. In mere days the Padre's message got their response; chiefs and couriers came with the information. The blue shells from the Yumans could not come from the Gulf because the blue-crusted abalone didn't occur in those dense waters. They had been traded hand to hand from the distant Pacific. Obviously, California was not an island, but Kino needed to prove it on foot.

In early May a flurry of letters expressing Kino's opinions about a "royal road" to California were sent throughout the province. Encouragement for a new expedition came from all quarters. On September 24, 1700, Padre Kino and ten Indians departed from Dolores; destination: the Colorado. He angled northwest along a more direct path to Gila Bend, making new

friends as he went. In twelve days he had arrived at the village of San Pedro where he had been the previous year with Padre Gilg and Manje.

One wonders why Kino pressed on to the Colorado alone. Perhaps his trail companions were too busy or too weary of gruelling expeditions. Perhaps they no longer shared Kino's vision of the importance of a land route to California. But one must also suspect that Kino wasn't anxious to risk the lives of others in stepping off into the unknown. The Pimas, he knew; the Cocomáricopas, he trusted; but the Yumans somehow called for caution uncharacteristic of Kino. Did their resemblance to the Californians trigger earlier fears?

Alone and nearly three hundred miles from help he climbed a peak at the tip of the Gila range and surveyed the Colorado delta with a

15

long-range telescope. He was on the edge of a vast valley that could swallow him without a trace. His Pima guides were queasy about their situation, and besides, the round-up had to get under way if cattle were to be sent to California. The long range survey was done and the pack train was turned back up the Gila. But in the slanting shadows of late afternoon the Yumas caught up with Padre Kino on the trail.

If he didn't postpone the return, he was certain to offend the sensitive and powerful Yuman people. It was a double dilemma between time and fright. Tossing caution to the winds and letting his customary optimism be his guide, Padre Eusebio smiled at the insistent, tearful Indians and agreed to go to their village on the Colorado. He rose before dawn, celebrated Mass and cantered downriver, coming across clusters of Indians who had traveled through the night to meet him on the trail. His horse's gait slowed with each mile as the welcoming throng grew. By noon he rode into the huge Yuma town where over a thousand Indians greeted him in peace. Within another day some five hundred more arrived and word came that hundreds were on their way from north and south along the Colorado! The Yumans were gigantic in stature, and one of them was the largest Indian Kino had ever seen. It must have been a little nerve-wracking to be the willing captive of such giants. But Padre Kino's own good will and understanding of the Indian ways won a whole new nation in friendship. His duties at Dolores called and he had to leave, but he promised a return — soon. On the homeward route he climbed yet another peak and saw the head of the Gulf glistening in an October sunset. The devil himself must have been grumbling as Kino turned his trail of death into a highway of conquest.

Padre Juan María Salvatierra in the meanwhile had not been idle. His new mission at Loreto in Baja California desperately needed supplies from the mainland. So the industrious missionary crossed the Gulf and scouted the harbor of Guaymas for a new mission and seaport site. Salvatierra had gotten Kino's reports on the shells and the trek to the Colorado. He was shipping cattle to California by sea at a cost of $300 a head; even the worst desert in the world would offer a cheaper route. By late February both Salvatierra and Manje were rapping at the door of Kino's adobe in Dolores. It had been five years since they were in Mexico and ten since they rode the Pimería together discussing the future of the missions.

Another expedition west was in the making. But Padre Kino had first to attend to the fortification of the mountain missions since the Apaches were opening a new and bold campaign of attack all along the Sierra Azul chain. Knowing Piman fluently from his days as a missionary in Chínipas, Salvatierra went on ahead preaching his way through the valley of the Río Magdalena. A week later Kino joined the party at Caborca and they set out for Sonoita where provisions had been forwarded. This time the explorers were determined to bypass the Devil's Highway and find a direct route to the mouth of the Colorado.

What might have been one of the most significant expeditions of the careers of both Kino and Salvatierra was bungled by a half-wit Indian guide. Apparently that summer guides were at an unpayable premium; already some had refused to disclose watering places on the trail up from Caborca. Salvatierra wanted to go due west from Sonoita which would have brought them north of Pinacate into impassable sand dunes. Kino listened to the Indian guides who favored a passage south of Pinacate. Manje argued for the only rational path — the Devil's Highway.

Kino prevailed and they turned south around Pinacate onto the horrifying volcanic mesa spewed out by the burned-out mountain. All Salvatierra could think of was what the world would look like after the final ordeal by fire. All they encountered — save for a few destitute Indians and a withered centenarian — were ashes, boulders, and sand. Water became a critical problem, particularly for the animals. The guides recommended a trail along the Gulf shore, so they inched across the searing boulders and sand. For three days they searched out a way; it was hopeless. The water at Tres Ojitos just north of modern Puerto Peñasco was insufficient and the remainder of the pack train they had left at the foot of Pinacate had to be brought back to water. Reluctantly they turned back.

Having replenished their supplies at Sonoita they set out again toward the north, but the Pima guides refused to enter into Yuman territory. It was a bad show all around. But the trio did manage to climb a steep, high peak north of Pinacate and from its heights they viewed a sunset glinting on the not so distant California mountains. Salvatierra was satisfied, but Kino and Manje were disgruntled. By violating their unwritten law of conquering the tierra incógnita by known quantities, they lost the marvelous opportunity to link the Californias inseparably to the Pimería during their lifetimes.

Word spread through the Pimería of the new confirmations of Kino's discoveries. Another expedition was planned by the indefatigable trio for October. But Salvatierra had to beg off because Mission Loreto in California lacked horses to explore the west side of the Gulf. Manje was caught in a reshuffling of policy when General Jironza retired at the end of the summer, so Kino was left holding the reins all alone.

Padre Eusebio invited a Spaniard to accompany him on the next trip to the Colorado. He left Dolores on November 3, 1701, and remaining resourceful as ever, found another new route across the Papaguería as far as San Pedro on the Gila. Hundreds of Yumans and Pimans thronged around the Blackrobe just as they had done the year before. Kino was in his element, but as the cavalcade moved south along the Colorado, fear gripped his traveling companion. A full quarter hour had elapsed before Padre Kino realized the poor Spaniard had ridden off in terror of his life. Two Pima cowhands chased after him on the fastest horses in the train, but they could not catch the timid, terrified man. No doubt he would hatch some choice rumors to exonerate his cowardice. Well, it wouldn't be the first time rumors reached the Pimería that Kino had been eaten alive by angry savages.

Padre Kino was touched in observing that the Yumas and the Quíquimas were fascinated by the celebration of the Mass. He was amused by their reaction to the horses and mules which they had never seen before. When the Quíquimas were told that horses could run faster than the Indians, they scoffed incredulously. So the Dolores cowboys arranged a race and the fleet footed Quíquimas dashed ahead of the ambling horses; then the spurs were put to their flanks and the galloping steeds passed the astonished aborigines in a victorious cloud of dust.

The horses may have been excellent for exploration, but they needed to have the brush cleared away in order to negotiate the river lands. It was obvious they couldn't swim the swift Colorado. Yet the Quíquimas insisted that Kino visit their lands on the opposite bank. Nothing could be more agreeable because Kino hoped to reach the shores of the great South Sea still ten days to the west.

Dry timbers were lashed together for a raft and the horses were led toward the shaky craft; however, the horses mired down and shied from the strange surface of rippling timbers. Even Padre Kino was reluctant to get his boots wet — not because he was fastidious, but he knew too well how essential good footgear is to the desert explorer. The Indians fastened a large waterproof basket on the raft and Kino carefully sat down in his private compartment for the historic crossing of the Colorado.

His sojourn in Quíquima land was brief but hospitable. He had to return to Dolores because the Spaniard who deserted him might cause untold troubles for the Indians of the west should the garrison at Real de San Juan or Fronteras mount a search for a "missing" Padre Kino. At least Kino was now absolutely sure the Gulf ended to the south of the juncture of the Gila and the Colorado and that a land route to Loreto was possible. Back on the east bank of the river the Padre was laden with two hundred loads of foodstuffs as gifts from the Quíquimas. What he gratefully accepted he graciously gave to the needy Yumas whose crops had failed that year.

The news of the crossing of the Colorado hardly jolted the Pimería, now accustomed to the rapid advances made by the aging Padre on horseback. Everyone realized the immense importance of a land route, but one suspects that the Indian raids along the whole northern perimeter were sapping the Spanish strength. No one could break free for the next entrada of 1702 except for Kino's old Jesuit stalwart, Padre Manuel González, who had first introduced Kino to the Pimería.

The cavalcade that formed at Dolores in early February was worthy of the two missionaries. One hundred and thirty horses and mules, laden with provisions, were the core. Kino would amplify that with some of the 1000 head of cattle at Síboda! The whole Spanish colony must have been dumbfounded to think that Padre Kino with one other priest-companion and a few cowhands from Dolores could move herds of animals in perfect peace across the open desert when they couldn't keep a goat or a mine secure for a month.

Padre González was a perfect trail companion. He was as warmly received as Kino and equally enthusiastic about the extensive mission foundations that could be set up on the Colorado. The pair directed the pack train south from San Dionisio and studied ways of crossing the immense river. The difficulties remained the same: the horses mired down and the rafts were useless. And to complicate the problems, Padre González became very ill. Pain and hardship were constant companions to any missionary, so the discomfort Padre González experienced along the trail was nothing out of the ordinary. But the long hours in the saddle had aggravated an old hemorrhoid condition, and the rugged travel and exposure to winter weather had not helped at all.

Padre Kino now realized it would be impossible to cross the river and penetrate to the Pacific coast. Nor could time be lost in getting González back to help. The urgency can be learned from the fact that Padre Kino turned due east from where he was on the Colorado. He committed himself to crossing the sand dunes of the *Gran Desierto*, the Sahara of Sonora. Howling winds lashed the company with stinging sand. The animals and men sank in the dry drifts making every step in advance an agony of frustration. They had fought their way nearly forty miles, about half-way to Pitaqui Peak, when they had to give up. They retraced their steps and turned back along the more reliable river trails. Padre González braved his painful condition down the Devil's Highway, to him now so appropriately named. Reaching Sonoita, he rested for three days but worsened. Loyal Pimas placed him on a litter and carried him back across the desolate Papaguería.

It was Padre Ignacio Iturmendi who met the desperate and now bedraggled cavalcade. González lingered between life and beckoning death; nothing brought him relief or strength. In a few days he died.

Curiously enough those three Fathers who met under such trying circumstances would all be dead within ten years, and each would lie buried in the same chapel for centuries awaiting discovery and the honors of historical fame.

The death of Padre González was a blow, but the loss did not lessen the importance of the expedition. The reality of a land passage to California was beyond a dream, and true. A mainland port on the Pacific could at last end the agony of anxiety which dogged the Manila galleon; it could mean naval supremacy for the whole hemispheric coast; it would halt the advance of Russia into the New World. And above all it would mean an earlier Christianization for the tens of thousands of Indians hunting and scrabbling out an existence in the chaparral of the Southwest.

Padre Eusebio Kino came back from the Colorado and settled down to the exhaustive routine of pueblo life. At fifty-six years old, it was time to slacken the pace. But Kino didn't understand life quite that way. The last ten years of his life set a staggering record for a man of any age. Even incomplete records of his expeditions give a total of over eight thousand miles on horseback through the most hostile desert on the continent. A day's ride continued to average well over 30 miles, not accounting for side trips to visit the sick, to instruct and baptize. With him he drove herds of cattle, sheep, goats, horses, and burros. How these animals were fed and watered was a problem that apparently only the genius of Kino could resolve.

Padre Kino was no longer on the brink of discovery. He had crossed the Colorado, charted the approaches to the California coast, criscrossed the head of the Gulf, and defied the Gran Desierto itself. While he unravelled rumor from fact in the western haze, the mission frontier behind him struggled to keep pace. Armies of carpenters, bricklayers, farmers, and irrigation experts swarmed through the pueblos updating and expanding the economy. A dream was coming true. Padre Kino had come to a desert. He came among abandoned peoples. He rode the arid trails. He bore the acid criticism of colonials. Why? Because he recognized that the paradox of Christianity is locked in the paradox of the desert. Life is more meaningful where life seems not to be. People are dearer where people seem they could not be. Peace is more possible where man recognizes the potentials of hostility.

The Pimería Alta had responded to the vision of Padre Eusebio. His dedication, his dreams, and his devotion had not changed the Pimería as much as it had brought it to life. But Padre Kino, like every man, had to come to the end of the trail . . .

With joy and gratitude in his heart Padre Eusebio rode into Magdalena in March, 1711. He had come to dedicate a new chapel to St. Francis Xavier — his personal patron and that of the Pimería. He began the Mass of dedication and during it fell desperately ill. Padre Campos helped the indomitable missionary to the modest priest's house where Indian friends milled about praying for his recovery.

Life lingered until midnight on that 15th day of March, then drifted away from the figure on the adobe floor. Kino died as he had lived — in peace and poverty, and on the brink of something greater.

Padre Campos chose the chapel for his burial place. And through the centuries since his death the village of Magdalena has been the center of an undiminishing devotion to St. Francis Xavier. For dozens of decades the faithful from Sonora, Arizona, and even Chihuahua have traveled hundreds of miles, many of them on foot, to participate in the fiesta of San Francisco. The reason baffles many people. But ethnologists offer a simple explanation: the Indians have simply transformed Padre Kino's devotion to San Francisco into one of mutual homage to the patron of the Pimería and to the pioneer padre himself. And who knows but what they're right?

The valley of the San Miguel at Mission Dolores

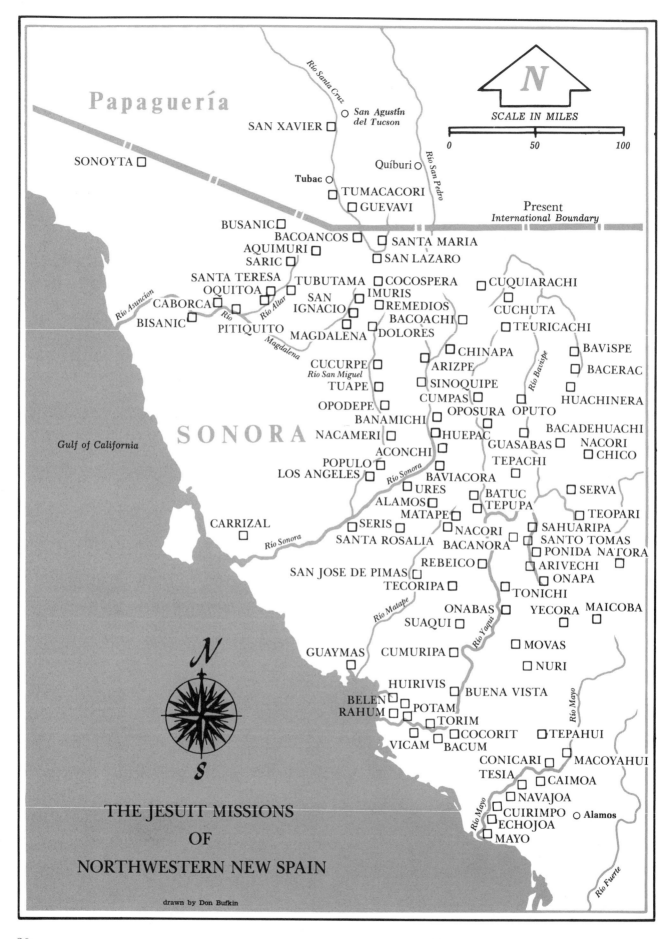

Papaguería

Río Santa Cruz

San Agustín
del Tucson

SAN XAVIER

SONOYTA

Quíburi

Río San Pedro

Tubac

Present
International Boundary

SCALE IN MILES

0   50   100

TUMACACORI

GUEVAVI

BUSANIC

BACOANCOS

SANTA MARIA

AQUIMURI

SARIC

SAN LAZARO

SANTA TERESA

OQUITOA

TUBUTAMA

COCOSPERA

CUQUIARACHI

Río Asunción

CABORCA

SAN
IGNACIO

IMURIS

REMEDIOS

CUCHUTA

Río

Río Altar

BACOACHI

TEURICACHI

BISANIC

PITIQUITO

MAGDALENA

DOLORES

Magdalena

BAVISPE

Río San Miguel

CUCURPE

CHINAPA

ARIZPE

BACERAC

Río Bavispe

TUAPE

SINOQUIPE

HUACHINERA

Gulf of California

OPODEPE

CUMPAS

OPOSURA

OPUTO

BANAMICHI

BACADEHUACHI

SONORA

NACAMERI

HUEPAC

GUASABAS

NACORI
CHICO

ACONCHI

TEPACHI

POPULO

LOS ANGELES

Río Sonora

BAVIACORA

SERVA

URES

ALAMOS

BATUC

TEPUPA

MATAPE

TEOPARI

CARRIZAL

SERIS

NACORI

SAHUARIPA

SANTO TOMAS

Río Sonora

SANTA ROSALIA

BACANORA

PONIDA NATORA

REBEICO

ARIVECHI

SAN JOSE DE PIMAS

ONAPA

TECORIPA

TONICHI

Río Matape

ONABAS

YECORA

MAICOBA

SUAQUI

Río Yaqui

GUAYMAS

CUMURIPA

MOVAS

NURI

HUIRIVIS

BUENA VISTA

Río Mayo

BELEN

RAHUM

POTAM

TORIM

COCORIT

TEPAHUI

VICAM

BACUM

CONICARI

MACOYAHUI

TESIA

CAIMOA

NAVAJOA

Río Mayo

CUIRIMPO

Alamos

ECHOJOA

MAYO

Río Fuerte

THE JESUIT MISSIONS

OF

NORTHWESTERN NEW SPAIN

drawn by Don Bufkin

20

THE PIMERIA ALTA BEFORE AND AFTER PADRE KINO

Padre Kino seems to stand as a lone giant on the unknown horizons of southwestern history. But this is more an illusion created by a climate of ignorance than an intentional distortion of historiography. Kino did not labor alone, nor were his accomplishments significant because of their singularity. Padre Kino was only one of many who devoted life and talent so that the Pimería might take its rightful place among nations. Kino's exploits gained prominence not because they were performed in a remote and isolated land but because they were the deeds of a most extraordinary man among extraordinary men. It would be unfair, an inaccuracy of history, to omit mention of others who worked before, with, and after Kino on this frontier. They shared at least a part of his vision, and they mutually shaped the fortunes of this land.

Jesuit mission expansion in northwestern New Spain had been rapid and successful. In 1591 two Blackrobes began work at the Villa of San Felipe near Culiacán, Sinaloa, and in less than a decade the mission frontier leaped northward from the river deltas into the mountain fastnesses of the Sierra Madre Occidental. Working systematically with an increasing number of men, the Jesuits reached the Río Yaqui in southern Sonora by 1617. In that quarter century the mission field had expanded from two priests serving hundreds in Sinaloa to more than thirty men ministering to thousands along the whole northwest coast.

Contact with the native peoples of central Sonora was made in 1621, but the momentum of mission expansion slowed considerably after 1626 when the great frontier captain Don Diego Martínez de Hurdaide retired from service. Civil and military affairs were entrusted to Don Pedro de Perea, who had distinctly different ideas about frontier expansion and exploitation. Perea soon settled on a plan to carve out a new kingdom, Nueva Andalusia, over which he would rule. His personal attention focused on the remote valley of the Río Sonora, above the great bend near Ures. This lush, desert valley was ideal for farming and ranching; the flanking hills cloaked rich veins of silver and gold. Perea chose the valley as the site of his hacienda and brought his wife, Doña María Ibarra, to Banámichi. Fearing the influence of the Jesuit missionaries over the Indian populace of the valley, Don Pedro invited five Franciscans from New Mexico into central Sonora. Already claiming the establishment of several missions throughout the area, the Jesuits confronted Perea and challenged his intentions.

In 1645 Perea determined to send the gray-robed friars of St. Francis into the unevangelized territory of the Hýmeris, as the Pimas Altas were then known. An expedition was prepared to enter the land but Perea was taken violently ill on July 31, the feast of St. Ignatius. He reluctantly returned to Tuape. In a few weeks he recovered and set out again with the same intentions, but he took sick again and died on October 4, the feast of St. Francis Assisi! It would almost seem that the founders of the two orders were being drawn into this Sonoran rivalry.

Perea's death plunged the province into turmoil. The Jesuits urged their exclusive claim to operate missions throughout Sonora, and the Franciscans acquiesced by agreeing to leave Sonora in 1650. Immediately the Jesuits prepared to move deep into the Pimería Alta; Padres Pedro Bueno and Francisco París were selected as the emissaries to the new conversions among the Pimas. But just as their cavalcade started into the territory, the new military commander at the Real of San Juan Bautista, Don Juan de Peralta, ordered the entry to be stopped. Officially the Jesuits lost the much awaited chance to open new missions among the Pimas, but quite miraculously the pack animals of the cavalcade wandered throughout the Pimería and returned unscathed. Officialdom may have hardened the "Rim of Christendom" for a few years, but the burros of the Blackrobes had a good glimpse of a mission field that would have to wait for the coming of Padre Kino thirty-seven years later.

With the passing of Perea new policies and directions came to Sonora. Prospectors filtered

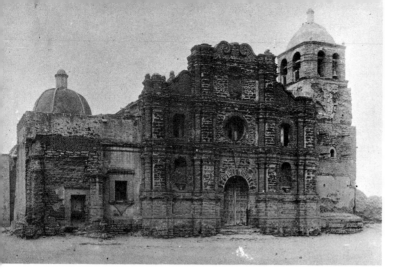

Jesuit Mission Headquarters—Oposura, Sonora

into the harsh canyons searching for rich pockets of precious metals. Like most soldiers of fortune these *gambusinos* had little time left to care for themselves so they acquired food, clothing, and supplies on whatever credit might be extended. At this time in Sonoran history a remarkable Jesuit from Sardinia, Padre Daniel Angelo Marras, was assigned to San José de Mátape, the mission at the end of the Camino Real. Marras arrived just soon enough to learn the fine points of the Nébome language from Padre Lorenzo Cárdenas, the organizer of the upper Sonoran missions. Cárdenas died in 1656, leaving Mátape in the care of the young, enterprising Marras. His Indian mission was in the heart of the silver country, and it was to him the gambusinos came to beg supplies.

If any single missionary changed the face of Sonora, it was Padre Daniel. Coming into a newly organized frontier, he recognized the critical position of the native communities. Quickly he won the admiration of the people and transformed the new missions into productive, agricultural centers. He begged and bartered for 600 head of breeding stock from the lower Sinaloan missions. By the time of Marras' reassignment to Puebla in 1681, he had increased the herd to over 50,000!

The ranches under Marras' administration were so productive that cattle drives were initiated from Sonora to Mexico City in the 1680's. The industry that later became a distinguishing mark of Sonora was actually the stepchild of Padre Daniel, yet almost no one remembers or even knows of him. Agricultural production increased so much that Spanish farmers in the region accused him of overproduction and undercutting their inflated markets. And the wandering prospectors became so indebted that one man was obliged to sign over his properties to Mátape; in this curious manner Marras was plunged into the tumultuous business of mining and refining silver. Although critics have accused the missionaries of engaging in mining, which was strictly forbidden by the rules of the religious orders, Marras actually accepted mining claims in payment for debts owed to the *college* of Mátape, not the mission. These acquisitions were completely permissible, but historical vagueness has confused the affair. Subsequent rectors of the college of Mátape were ordered to sell the properties, which took several years because the region remained so depressed; no one was able to buy. The cunning Sardinian of Sonora had witnessed some of Sonora's most prosperous days.

Only five years after Marras' departure Padre Kino arrived in the Pimería Alta to take advantage of the fertile land and industrious native settlements. Essentially Kino did exactly as Marras had done—he also begged breeding stock and increased them into the tens of thousands. Most of the Sonoran missionaries benefitted from the solid foundations Marras laid down, although few were as successful as Marras or Kino in the north. Padre Adam Gilg struggled to convert the simple, nomadic Seris, but neither land nor people were suited to industrious expansion. Padre Marcos de Loyola at San Ignacio de Cuquiarachi held the precarious line between Opatas and Apaches; his situation held little hope for new conversions. To the north and west Padre Kino found inviting opportunities; he met the challenge with imagination and determination.

Kino shared the Pimería Alta with several missionaries. Probably the foremost among them was Padre Agustín de Campos who arrived in the early years of its development. In 1693, just after taking his final vows in the Society, Campos was assigned to San Ignacio de Caborica, near Magdalena. While Kino pushed farther toward the western reaches of the desert, Padre Agustín tended the missions of the heartland along the Magdalena and Santa María rivers. Quiet and stoic, Campos has received little recognition from history. His journeys probably gave many Arizona sites their place names. Even Tucson preserves the patronage of St. Augustine and the Catalina Mountains the faint memory of a Mass he once celebrated in a Piman village at their foot. Although Kino has been remembered for his extensive explorations, Campos rode the limits of the same frontier and penetrated the White Mountains in search of the Moqui. Kino spent twenty-four years putting the Pimería on the map; Campos spent forty-three years keeping it there. He frequently performed duty as chaplain to the hard-riding flying company of Sonora. Weeks on the trail made him a fast friend of Captain Juan Bautista de Anza, father of the colonizer of San Francisco. His last days were spent in the quiet of the Anza home at Fronteras, until he went reluctantly to Chihuahua where he died.

The first decade after Kino's death was difficult for the Pimería Alta. Manpower continued to be scarce and the apostolic commitments did not dwindle. Kino's old mission of Dolores remained the headquarters for far-ranging visits. The recently established Christian communities in old Indian pueblos deserved at least an occasional visit from a missionary. San Xavier del Bac, Tubutama, Santa María Suamca, and Caborca had no resident missionaries. Fathers José Tenorio and Luis Velarde, who had replaced the aged and the dead, worked desperately to maintain the mountain missions; Campos continued to ride the circuit in the desert valleys. The hectic situation prevailed for nearly a decade until Father Luis Gallardi arrived at Caborca. A change of policy was breathing new life into the beleaguered frontier. Since 1707, when the Jesuit administration was ruled by short-sighted perfectionists, the missions and the Indian neophytes suffered terribly; even the last years of Kino's life felt the harshness of restrictive orders that banned his explorations and expansion. By 1721 Father Luis Marciano was assigned to Tubutama, and slowly the Pimería Alta was being knit together for a new surge of evangelization of the late 1720s. Bishop Benito Crespo visited the northern tier of missions in his diocese of Durango in 1727, urging more missionaries to serve the growing Christian communities. King Felipe V responded to Crespo's suggestions by ordering the Viceroy to support new efforts in the Pimería Alta.

The 1730s saw the first new wave of missionaries break over the desert lands. Some of them showed a vitality and optimism reminiscent of Padre Kino himself. The first of the new group was Father Gaspar Stiger, a Swiss from Oberried (St. Gallen), who came to San Ignacio in 1731 to be tutored in the Pima dialects by the accomplished Father Campos. And when Campos relinquished his post in 1736, after forty-three years of service, Stiger took charge of San Ignacio, remaining there until his death in 1762. While Padre Stiger studied the Piman languages at San Ignacio, another Swiss and two German missionaries arrived for assignment to long vacant missions.

Strategically located, the mission of Santa María de los Pimas (Suamca) became the base of operations for Father Ignacio Keller. This gruff Moravian shortly undertook expeditions down the San Pedro, hoping like Campos, to link up with the Moqui villages of the north. On one hapless trip Keller and his Piman escorts were stripped of all their horses and supplies after they had crossed the Gila in Apache country. Sheer stamina and courage protected them from total annihilation. As Keller approached a quarter century of service he found himself in the middle of a bitter controversy in which he was accused of triggering the bloody Pima rebellion of 1751, a story that will be told below.

The other Swiss missionary to join in the revitalized efforts in the Pimería Alta was Father Philip Segesser, a nobleman of Lucerne. He was assigned to San Xavier del Bac, the largest Piman settlement in the region and also the most distant from the Spanish perimeter of defense. Permanent residency here had been nearly impossible since Kino's founding of the mission in 1700. Segesser himself spent only a little more than a year in this fertile mission before he was recalled to Los Santos Angeles de Guevavi where Father Johann Grazhofer had died under mysterious circumstances. Some years after Grazhofer's death an old Indian resident of Guevavi claimed that he had poisoned the missionary, but there is strong reason to doubt this since Grazhofer had been seriously ill with a fever he contracted on his way to the Pimería Alta. Remaining at Guevavi for about a year, Segesser then left for work in the missions of central Sonora.

Vacant for several years after the death of Father Ignacio Iturmendi, the mission of Tubutama reestablished its importance as a mission center in 1721 with the coming of Father Luis Marciano and later Luis Gallardi. They set the stage for the revitalization of the western Pimería in the 1730s, especially with the arrival of Father Jacob Sedelmayr. Taking charge of Tubutama in 1736 Sedelmayr witnessed great transformations in the frontier apostolate. Campos was removed from San Ignacio; Gallardi died after sixteen years of work at Caborca and Tubutama; San Xavier del Bac and Guevavi were still vacant. And Padre Sedelmayr was left alone at a post that demanded a vigorous missionary.

Sedelmayr was cut from the same cloth as Kino. He travelled extensively and looked on the Pimería with a progressive optimism that had been missing among the missionaries for many years. Once again pack trains moved with regularity across the Papaguería to the missions on the Colorado. Exploring upward on the wide red river, Sedelmayr reached the edges of Moqui country. Analysis of his travel diaries seems to indicate that he reached the Bill Williams River which he followed into central Arizona. The entradas of this blond-haired German were part of a concerted Jesuit effort to establish missions along the Gila and Colorado. The official attitude on mission expansion in the 1740s had changed dramatically, but the quarter-century slow-down was difficult to overcome. The advances, however, were obliterated by the disastrous Pima rebellion of 1751.

The Pimería had been remarkably peaceful for three generations with the exception of the limited uprising in 1695. The climate for rebellion was probably created in the tumultuous 1730s when the Pimería Alta once again came to life under the ambitious Alcalde Mayor Baron Gabriel Prudhón de Beltrán Heider y Mújica. During his administration emphasis on exploiting the mineral wealth of the province attracted adventurers and soldiers of fortune to the desert frontiers. In 1736 a Yaqui Indian, Antonio Sirumea, stumbled onto a massive concentration of virgin silver in an arroyo west of the Cíbuta Valley near a Piman settlement named Arizonac. Once word of the discovery reached the interior of Sonora hundreds of hopeful colonials converged on the arid region. Some were fortunate enough to find large slabs of silver—one weighing as much as 2,500 pounds! Appalled by the discovery, the Jesuit missionaries could only see this as the occasion for an invasion of "the dregs of humanity" into mission lands. A strong case was made that the silver was not virgin, but that it had indeed been mined earlier by Spaniards or even Aztecs on their way to Mexico! The Jesuits insisted that the discovery was actually a treasure; in this way the law would deliver the silver to the Crown and block the immigration of opportunistic colonials. Bitter experience for a century and a half showed that Indian unrest soon followed the intrusive presence of mining camps.

The Jesuits' fears were not exaggerated because within fifteen years the unruly mining camps had introduced envy, hatred, ambition and anarchy into the Indian pueblos. Despite vehement protests by the missionaries the Spanish governor for Sonora appointed a haughty Pima, Luis Oacpicagigua (Luis of Sáric), as the responsible Indian governor of the Pimas Altos. Luis had served with presidial forces in campaigns against the Seris on the Gulf coast. He knew the strengths and weaknesses of the Spanish military. Within months of his appointment as Indian governor he organized a coordinated uprising of Pimas against the Spanish reales (mining towns) and missions. Scores of Spaniards were slaughtered and the mission put under seige. Padre Sedelmayr was wounded by a poisoned arrow at Tubutama, but recovered and escaped to the south. Not so Father Tomás Tello who was cut down at Caborca and Father Henrique Ruhen who was martyred on a desert trail near his mission of Sonoita. Before the Spaniards could react the whole of the Pimería was pillaged and left smouldering in ruin.

The rebellion itelf was put down in a relatively short time, four months, but its effects rippled through the ensuing decade. In one sense its effects reached permanently into the future because the Spanish policy shifted in favor of a strong military presence. Presidios were stationed at Altar and Tubac, the latter being the place where the rebellion flared on a cold November morning in 1751. The small garrisons were designed to keep the Pimas in line, but the unrest and injustices that had triggered the rebellion also broke the loose tribal alliances among the Pimans themselves. With this disintegration the Spanish first line of defense against the Apache crumbled, and it was only a matter of time before the nomadic marauders had pushed deep into Sonoran territory.

Under cover of Spanish cavalry the missionaries returned to their demolished churches to rebuild and start anew. Even though the frontier remained unsettled, a large new church was begun at San Xavier del Bac. In 1756 the new Governor of Sonora Don Juan Antonio de Mendoza laid the first adobe in place for the mission church. (Two hundred and ten years later archaeologists found its forgotten foundations just a hundred feet west of the imposing baroque successor.) A new roster of missionaries filtered into the vacancies along the frontier as an optimistic future dawned once again for the Pimería. Explorations in the next decade were less bold because the rebellion had taught unfriendly Indians to be more brash. Nevertheless the Blackrobes rode to the distant Colorado and all along the Gila to visit the Christian communities that still remained faithful.

Twenty-two missions far to the south in Sinaloa and Durango were turned over to the Bishop as part of a plan of secularization. The transfer of responsibility released several Jesuits for new missions planned in Alta California, but the plans remained just that, plans. In 1767 the entire Jesuit missionary program was snapped like a brittle branch from the dying tree of the Spanish empire. By order of Charles III, the less than enlightened monarch of all the Spains, every Jesuit throughout the Spanish empire, more than 5,000 of them, was banished. With lightning swiftness each Jesuit missionary, teacher, and public servant was arrested and bound over to regional authorities for exile to Spain and other European countries. Native-born Jesuits were exiled from their homelands and scattered about in foreign countries. In many ways the expulsion of the Society of Jesus from Portugal, France, and Spain, and its eventual suppression in 1773 was one of the more curious events of the eighteenth century.

No area under Spanish control was exempt from the King's decree which was executed in every case by the highest officials of the empire under the unusual penalty of death for failure to comply. The Pimería Alta like Patagonia and the Philippines fell under the pall of Bourbon intrigue. In Sonora the Jesuits were taken without previous warning and escorted in chains to the dilapidated college at Mátape in the south central part of the province. In the steamy heat of July fifty-five former missionaries were gathered in the chapel where the decree of banishment was read; under cautious military guard the Blackrobes were marched down the sandy river to the seaport of Guaymas.

By early August the embargo that Visitador General José de Gálvez had placed on the West coast had taken full effect. No ship was ready to transport the Jesuits to San Blas, so they were confined to a stone warehouse usually employed for storing supplies bound for Baja California. For nine months the men were crowded in the small building without being allowed outside for exercise. By May, 1768, the men were deathly sick, but relief came when a small French packet-boat arrived to take them into exile.

Their release from confinement was short lived, however, because spring storms clutched the sailing vessel and blew it across the Gulf to Puerto Escondido. There the dying Jesuits were confined to the now becalmed ship because Spanish officials feared reprisals from Visitor General Gálvez if they were allowed to land. Finally at the insistence of Fray Junípero Serra, the newly installed Franciscan superior of the missions, Governor Gaspar de Portolá broke down and permitted them to be brought ashore for rest and better care. For two weeks the Jesuits continued to improve, but as soon as news arrived that Gálvez was only two days away the still sickly refugees were forced back on the ship

which sailed immediately. Landing at San Blas the once vigorous missionaries dropped in death as their forced march carried them from the tropical coast to the highlands of Guadalajara. Twenty died under the extreme exertion — including Juan Nentwig of Guásavas, Manuel Aguirre of Bacadéguachi, and Pedro Díez of Atil.

Had the officials of Guadalajara not intervened to stop the brutal mistreatment of the Sonoran Jesuits, the toll would have been appreciably higher. But their plight was immediately recognized and Gálvez who was far away in California could not intervene. There would be no danger for the powerful members of the Audiencia to order carriages for the weakened survivors. Their trip continued through Mexico City to Vera Cruz where ships took them off to Europe.

Reaching Europe was no return to Paradise. The exiled Jesuits, if from foreign nations, were interrogated and sent back to their home countries. In many cases a lack of funds or the conditions of war prevented repatriation. The royal answer to the dilemma of the unwelcome Jesuits was imprisonment on the second floor of the former hostel at Puerto Santa María across the bay from Cádiz. Several were never allowed out of confinement for as much as eight years! Eventually the last Jesuits were banished from Spain; most of the homeless sought refuge in Bologna, northern Italy. The great majority of them died there and were buried in a potter's field—including the famous Mexican historian Francisco Clavijero.

The expulsion of the Society of Jesus drew the curtain on the drama of Jesuit missionary activity in northwestern New Spain. It left the whole of the country with the skills of the Society's teachers, scientists, missionaries, and explorers. Valiantly the Franciscans tried to fill the vacuum left in the Pimería and in California. But the dispersal of the friars only thinned the ranks of already overworked missionaries. It was a task beyond the resources of the church of New Spain. A score of years of adjustment and adaptation passed before a burst of enthusiasm and splendor broke over the desert lands. Beginning in the 1780s impressive new missions sprung up on old Jesuit sites. Friars and soldiers closed ranks in probing the forbidding desert in search of reliable routes to the growing province of California.

The fresh hope that characterized the close of the eighteenth century was short lived. Within a scant forty years the whole venture approached collapse. Apache raids had ripped the northern frontier asunder; economic decline threatened the dependent mission system. And to top it all Spain fell victim to the expansionist demands of Napoleon Bonaparte. As Old Spain crumpled under the emperor's heel, New Spain raised the cry of independence. Mexico was reborn. But the new political freedom only assured that the lack of funds and concerns would shrivel the frontier that belonged to a deceased empire. Northwestern deserts held no attraction for the sophisticated politics of the new nation.

The Anglo-Americans who entered this land in mid-nineteenth century were puzzled by the ruins of an obviously splendid civilization. They swiftly annexed the vast land of mountains, deserts, rivers, canyons, volcanoes and beautiful bays. Its history was vague; its monuments, massive; and its potentials were staggering and unfulfilled. No wonder myths and legends sprouted to explain these anomalies in the desert West. Modern history has been left the task of explaining to contemporary man that these desert lands have not always been a wilderness void of importance. Quite to the contrary, they have been the scene of history-making events and the home of bold explorers who had opened new worlds to an empire already sated with discovery.

What modern America has learned about this land is not only that it had a fascinating history, but also that the visions of her pioneers were more realistic and perhaps even more challenging for our times than for theirs. The true treasures of the Pimería—her agricultural and recreational potentials, are still untouched. The curious thing about this land is not that it has had a history few have heard about, but that the past visions of her future are still unfulfilled. Kino would not be amazed at how much we have done, but at how little and how poorly we have dealt with this splendor of creation.

THE PIMERIA ALTA: FRANCISCANS AND AFTER

The world-wide Spanish empire was stunned by the sudden expulsion of the Society of Jesus in 1767. Blackrobes were everywhere, doing everything, and their swift removal left simple folk and sophisticates confused and disbelieving. Charles III's unexplained, secretive order rocked every frontier in the Americas. Sonora and the Pimería Alta were no exception. But such are the decisions of absolutists.

For decades the frontier missions had depended on missionaries for stability and direction. Entry and assimilation into Spanish society was not easy. Although the primary goal of the mission program envisioned the peaceful transition of native communities into full-fledged Spanish towns, that transition came slowly and with difficulty. Not all loyal subjects of the Crown were as willing to wait as the missionaries because opportunities to exploit land and labor diminished as long as the missions held sway. When the decree of expulsion came, many Spanish colonists cheered the news. In the name of the Enlightenment new freedom was finally being given the Indians.

In New Spain the change of policy was championed by Visitador General José de Gálvez, one of the most trusted and influential friends of Charles III. His task was to spearhead reforms being pressed by the Bourbons of Europe. And in his estimation the Jesuits were the single most effective threat to those changes. Gálvez was consumed by hate for the Blackrobes he considered as too powerful and too worldly. Far more to his personal liking were the men of the Order of Friars Minor; their religious spirit and ascetical practice conformed to his idea of how reforms had to be achieved. The Viceroy, the Marquis de Croix staunchly agreed.

When the decree of expulsion was issued, Gálvez and Teodoro de Croix the viceroy's nephew lost no time in enlisting the aid of Vice Commissary General Fray Manuel de Nájera to assign some fifty Franciscan replacements for the missions of the northwest. Nájera complied with Gálvez's directive because he really had no

alternative. Little did he realize the devastating change in mission policy that Charles III and Gálvez had devised. In the fashion of the times Gálvez appealed to Nájera's predilection for purely spiritual administration. Temporal management of the missions would become a function of civil officials. Mission communities would become villages of Spanish citizens willing and able to pay taxes, traffic with Spanish merchants, and take their place in the new society.

Therefore Nájera quickly sent orders to the apostolic colleges the Franciscans operated in New Spain. Volunteers responded enthusiastically. By September, 1767, forty-seven gray and blue robed friars had gathered near Tepic for transfer to the northwest and Baja California. It would be a marvelous new epoch in mission history now that the entrenched enemies of God and Church had been dislodged. The missions of Sonora and the Pimería were waiting.

Gálvez had made it quite clear that the Franciscans were only to minister to the spiritual needs of native communities. They were to leave all temporal administration to other appointed Spanish officials. The mission lands were being registered in the names of individual Indians, entered on the tax rolls, and distributed among eager colonials. All the financial holdings of the mission societies were confiscated and given to the Royal Treasury. The Indians themselves were no longer obliged to a day or two of communal labor as had been their tradition since pre-hispanic days. Rather, they were only to work for pay, or not at all. They were to forsake their native languages and use Spanish alone. No longer were Spaniards restricted from living in their mission towns, as free intercourse was encouraged. Every Indian would be a completely free citizen of the new society. And the Franciscans' task was to make this all happen.

By mid-winter the first of the friars from the Apostolic College of the Holy Cross at Querétaro had arrived in the Pimería Alta. The trip had been exhausting for many and the desert frontier was anything but hospitable. Fray Diego

Martín García walked to San Ignacio; Fray Juan Díaz rode to Caborca. And Fray Juan Crisóstomo Gil de Bernabé went north to Guevavi. Gil and Díaz as well as a later arrival Fray Francisco Hermenegildo Garcés each within a few years would pay with their lives for the enlightened policies of Gálvez and Croix.

Throughout the first half of 1768 the rest of the Querétaran contingent arrived at their posts. Fray Joseph Soler took over Ati very close to his companion Fray Joseph del Río at Tubutama. Fray Joseph Agorreta tried his hand at the struggling new mission of Sáric. And the hardest job of all fell to Fray Francisco Roche whose mission was Suamca.

Santa María de los Pimas, or Suamca, was situated in the pleasant valley at the headwaters of the Río Santa María (Santa Cruz). It had been the almost lifelong headquarters of the controversial Jesuit missionary Padre Ignacio Keller. Keller had figured prominently in the disastrous Pima rebellion of 1751, so the mission had known the ravages of Indian wrath whether Apache or Piman. Roche's assignment to Suamca would be genuine frontline duty on a shaky frontier. It did not take long before he was put to the test.

An exemplary Franciscan, Fray Francisco took up residence at Suamca in June; the natives of the community were unimpressed by his commitment to poverty. Their desires lay in other directions. Sensing a discontinuity of purposes—probably due to the worldly influence of the Blackrobes, Roche retreated to Cocóspera for a brief period. By November, however, he bravely returned to Suamca where he was caught in a savage attack by Apache raiders. Luckily he escaped with his life, but poor Suamca never rose again from the ashes of its destruction. There was a message in all of this, but no one heard.

Down river to the north Roche's companion, Fray Francisco Gracés, found San Xavier del Bac much to his liking. Moreover, the newly instituted policy of Gálvez was equally pleasing because he did not have to spend boring hours in the administration of the temporal affairs of the mission. Better to ride the trails of the western deserts than lock horns with neighboring Spaniards over Indian land and labor. Through the next decade Garcés stitched his name prominently in the fabric of history by crossing and recrossing the trails of the western desert. His treks carried him beyond Yuma to the Mojave and northwest to California. As many have said, he was the Franciscan answer to Padre Kino.

The Pimería, both Alta and Baja, put the apostolic mettle of all the Franciscans to strenuous test. By Gálvez's plan they had been stripped to near impotence in the administration of the missions. They were without means of discipline or encouragement. Each friar received 360 pesos annually from the King as his stipend. Although many had complained loudly that the Blackrobes had misappropriated their salaries to themselves, it became painfully obvious that the exiled missionaries had never been guilty of such accusations, in fact they had been marvelous managers in a decrepit and outmoded system that never corresponded to reality. Every member of the Franciscan replacement team complained bitterly to the college at Querétaro. Something would have to be done quickly or the whole effort would collapse as had many of the churches and conventos. For more than two years everything except administration of the sacraments was in the hands of civil commissaries—and they were the only ones profiting from control.

When the imperious Visitador General Gálvez finally returned to the mainland after a preposterous expedition to Baja California, he met missioner after missioner who pleaded for a change in policy. Even the megalomaniacal Gálvez had to agree. He relented by ordering that all the temporalities be returned to the control of the missionaries. Mission President Fray Mariano Buena y Alcalde breathed a little easier although he knew most of the moveable property had long been carried off by the interim commissarios. With all his power Gálvez would be no help because he now lapsed even more frequently into demented raving. Sonora's heat had not abated and the austerities of the frontier offered no solace. Fray Buena adroitly confined the Visitador to the mission at Ures where they tried to coax him to relax and recuperate. For several weeks Buena protected him from pressing correspondence and disturbing news. By

San José de Tumacácori—National Monument

late 1769 Gálvez was recovered enough to travel on to Chihuahua and Mexico City. Sonora was spared—at least for the time being.

The 1770s dawned amid profound political changes and rumors of more to come. The old familiar system of viceroys, kingdoms, and provinces was rewoven into an even more bureaucratic system of intendencies which had strong military overtones. Social and economic roles were streamlined to increase tax revenues and stress defense. Throughout Sonora and the Pimería Indian populations shrank with dread epidemics of contagious disease; peace was threatened in every sector. It was lucky for Gálvez that he was far distant because the situation might have snapped his mind permanently.

Charles III recalled the Visitador to Spain to take charge of the Council of the Indies. But Sonora still remained the focus of Gálvez's particular madness. From Madrid he raised isolated, thorn choked Arispe to the status of capital of the Provincias Internas, newly created as something less than a viceroyalty. He conspired with Fray Antonio de los Reyes to accept consecration as the first bishop of Sonora although Reyes was at complete odds with his Franciscan brothers. No small wonder that the work of the quiet friars on the frontier has been overshadowed by the intrigue and machinations of men in power.

Colonization and frontier defense dominated the minds of the policy makers. Frontier communities were drawn into the tangled purposes of global strategy. Fray Francisco Garcés was ordered to search out an overland route to the newly established California outposts—mission way stations along the military supply line to Monterey. Frontier-born Captain Juan Bautista de Anza rallied scores of hopeful

30

ranchers and adventurers to join him in incorporating Alta California into rejuvenated plans for expansion. Under the leadership of friars and soldiers the long arm of empire stretched northward to counter the Russian and English advances in North America. Theoreticians of expansion planned new towns, new commerce, new economies, and new routes of transport; people were merely pawns in a game of dreams. Unfortunately for Fray Garcés, three of his Franciscan companions and the dedicated Captain General Fernando Rivera y Moncada, the dream was a nightmare.

An expansionist euphoria had enveloped most of the Pimería Alta. Missionaries and military were agreed that the Indian populace had at last come to terms with change. Henceforth all would be peace and prosperity. Teodoro de Croix, Cabellero and Commandante General of the Provincias Internas, who ruled from Arispe in less than viceregal splendor, erected and erased presidial garrisons like a child with toy soldiers. And together with Fray Juan Díaz he designed a colony-mission on the banks of the Río Colorado—a place he had never seen, among a people he never understood. It was social planning gone mad.

Already the Yumas had grown short of food and supplies. How could they expect to refurbish expedition after expedition that braved the waterless deserts to cross the river where their ancient villages stood? The Spanish answer was simple and direct. A mission town would rise among the dunes. So, in the short daylight of December, 1780, long columns of Spanish immigrants reached Yuma crossing on the Colorado; the Indians perceived nothing but more problems. How were all these people and animals to be fed, watered, and housed? Where were the ever-present gifts by which other Spaniards had bribed their favor? Clearly these people had come to stay because straight streets were laid out in the shifting sand. Yuma might never be the same again.

It was a century after the tragic revolt of the Pueblos in New Mexico, and the Spaniards were pressing again. The natives took it for seven months. Then it became unbearable. In the sultry heat of July, 1781, the Yumas struck the un-suspecting Spaniards. Their two communities on either side of the vast river were totally destroyed. For a while the well known Fray Garcés was spared, but eventually all four Franciscan friars fell in the carnage. Angry hordes of Indians slaughtered the scattered platoons of soldiers; women and children were taken hostage. At any cost the Indians were determined to repossess their land and their way of life. It was a complete disaster. Over a hundred Spaniards lost their lives on the river where peace had reigned since Alarcón had first come two and a half centuries before.

Caballero Croix's essential link to California was severed. His social plan was a shambles. But he remained adamant that his unworkable schemes had only failed because of the incompetency of the friars and soldiers to whom he entrusted his programs. Still smarting from his reverses Croix left office in 1783 to accept promotion as the Viceroy of Peru; Charles III had an incredible record of rewarding paper politicians. As Croix left Arispe in viceregal splendor, Fray Antonio de los Reyes arrived in an episcopal

The ubiquitous Dolorosa.

31

pique. He had a plan for Sonora that was as unpopular and as unworkable as Croix's approach to frontier defense had been.

The missions of the Pimería Alta succumbed to ecclesiastical intrigue during the administration of Bishop Reyes. The new Commandante General of the partially reorganized Provincias Internas, Felipe de Neve, hardly had an opportunity to redirect the scattered efforts of Croix before he died. The Intendent of Sonora, Pedro de Corbalán, continued to the best of his abilities to achieve peace and equilibrium despite the pressures of the reformers. Reyes soon moved away from inconvenient Arispe to opulent Alamos. The missionaries of the Pimería he simply absorbed into his new diocese in a confusion of policy and purpose. Following the orders of Charles III, who himself followed the suggestions of Reyes, the Bishop established the Custodia of San Carlos, a new administrative district that would institute reforms in the mission communities. Nearly to a man the Franciscans fought Reyes' plan. The ecclesiastical counteroffensive was headed up by Fray Antonio de Barbastro, who finally won out against the first Bishop. Perhaps it was because Charles III had

died in the interim. Perhaps it was because Barbasto's arguments were clearly stronger. Who knows? But at least the missions and missionaries of the Pimería entered a whole new phase of development by the 1790s. Bishop Antonio de los Reyes never saw the surge of growth, passing on to his reward at Alamos in 1787.

One defiant Franciscan, Fray Juan Bautista de Velderrain, had determined that no ecclesiastical intrigue was going to deter him from building the finest church in the north. Velderrain had charge of San Xavier del Bac. And beneath the bishop's nose construction was begun on one of the most, if not the most, spectacular churches built during the period. Friars at Tubutama and Cocóspera and later at Caborca and Tumacácori caught construction fever; monuments in the desert grew upward despite the fiery rhetoric and early opposition.

Nuestra Señora del Pilar y Santiago de Cocóspera presents a prime example of controversy on the Sonoran frontier. Although Bishop Reyes had championed the idea of his Custodia of San Carlos, the Franciscans loyally looked to the apostolic college at Querétaro for independent assistance. Essentially this was the

J. Ross Browne's rendition of Cocóspera in 1864.

squabble between the Vice Custodian Barbastro and Bishop Reyes. Querétaro obliged the requests of Barbastro and continued to find and send volunteers to the mission frontier. One exemplary friar was Juan Antonio de Santiestevan, theology professor turned missionary. Fray Juan had come to the frontier in the early days of Reyes' new custodia; he long outlived the controversial Bishop and transformed the humble Jesuit adobes at Cocóspera into a finely sculpted church of brick and embellished neo-classic design. When Santiestevan retired, he left an elegant church in the hands of Fray Joaquín Goitia. But Cocóspera like all the missions on the frontier was coming up on the hard times of independence. The system that had brought them into existence and nurtured them over the years would shrivel in the echoes of the "Grito de Dolores" when Mexico gained its freedom from Napoleonic dominated Spain.

Without doubt Fray Barbastro had won the battle of mission policy—at least ecclesiastically. His position as President of the Pimería missions championed the old ways of winning native souls with temporal enducements. Generally speaking, the missions that were less exposed to hierarchical interference flourished; the communities more exposed to secular control disintegrated. Barbastro thought quite simply "by their fruits you shall know them." These policies held sway until 1795 when the winds of change blew out of Mexico City and Querétaro once again. The breeze arrived in the form of Fray Diego Miguel Bringas de Manzaneda y Encinas, appointed Visitor General to restructure the administration of the northwestern missions. Bringas blew in during the spring of 1795.

Despite his courtly name Bringas was a native Sonoran. Born at Alamos in 1762, he had been too young to have known the Blackrobes' missionary policy. When he arrived again in Sonora with the powers of visitor, he set out quickly to discover the problems that had infested the far flung communities. Rumors were rife that the Grayrobes were sliding into ill conceived practices and that the missions were bordering on corruption. Bringas recognized the rumors for what they were—rumors and criticisms born of greed and discontent. Nonethe-

less, he composed a striking report to the King, Charles IV, which never reached the Spanish court. In it he appealed for a staunch return to mission policies as they had been constituted before the reforms of Charles III. For The Pimería he wanted each of eight mission stations to maintain two resident friars; he also wanted them to be operated as *reducciones* without the presence of Spaniards in the communities. And having visited the whole frontier of the Pimería he recommended the establishment of several new missions including one at the junction of the Gila and Colorado where the colony of Croix had been annihilated.

His task completed, Friar Bringas left the Pimería Alta in the able hands of Fray Francisco Iturralde, a veteran of almost a score years in the northwest. As President of the missions Iturralde tried valiantly to mend the torn fabric of charity among dissident friars. He struggled to advance the cause of the missions among the still military-minded colonial officials. In many ways it appeared hopeless, but progress slowly became evident. The closing years of the 18th century were hard ones because the Spanish empire waned; English imperial ambitions waxed. France was ambivalent under Napoleon's nod. Who really could care for the needs of frontier missions when the purposes of power could be better served by war and the threats of war. Mission finance became even harder. Imperial policy sought out ever more stringent forms of taxation and revenue. President Fray Iturralde could only cringe at the absurd new demands for tithing the Indian communities.

The last gasp of greatness in the Pimería missions came in 1803 when Fray Andrés Sánchez broke ground for an impressive new church at Caborca. The other mission communities had relatively decent churches and conventos. Only Tumacácori and Caborca were substandard by early 19th century reckoning. The plan at Caborca would be nearly a duplication of San Xavier del Bac—only slightly larger and with more utilization of neo-classical embellishments. Energetic dedication made it possible to complete the church before the unforeseen Mexican War of Independence in 1810. Lucky for Caborca, because Tumacácori's less pretentious

structure was started later and work was suspended when imperial funds were cut off and local funds were exhausted.

With the War of Independence the northern frontiers suffered economic and social strangulation. The subsidized economies of the mission communities shrivelled. Military support and protection for the Indian programs almost completely ceased as loyalties divided and provincial factions vied for power. Precisely at the time the fledgling United States was consolidating power, New Spain was disintegrating as the Spanish empire crumbled under Napoleonic domination. To all intents and purposes the mission as an institution of social change ceased to function. Before its final disappearance the next two decades were denouement. The central themes of the drama had been played through; the principal actors were dead and gone. The few mission compounds that survived anywhere fulfilled only a custodial role in the decline of empire.

History pays attention only to the confusions of the struggle for power in Mexico and seldom treats of the collapse of the frontier. From 1810 onwards the frontier communities fought for recognition and identity. Loyalties were strained to the breaking point; support came from nowhere. The Franciscan college at Querétaro tried to maintain some semblance of commitment to the missions under its sway, but the college itself was plunged into political intrigue. Furthermore, the apostolic colleges had depended heavily on peninsular Spaniards to man the missions. In the search for independence most *peninsulares* were suspect, so the missions found themselves without financial subsidy or replacements.

When Mexico finally emerged as an independent imperial republic, there was a comparative period of stability. From 1821 through 1827 it appeared that the missions might regain their former strength. But the new spirit of nationalism swept through the people and the successful revolutionaries demanded the exile of all peninsulares. Few trusted the presence of the pure-blooded, Spanish born immigrant. The decree of expulsion hit the ranks of the religious orders particularly hard because many of the missionaries had come from Spain; it meant the immediate abandonment of scores of mission communities. In a few instances some peninsular priests were allowed to remain because of age or health.

Sonora was one of those provinces whose missionary team was mostly Spanish. Only two friars were left to care for the vast desert land. It was an impossible task by any standard. The Mexican federal congress on December 20, 1827 passed the law expelling the peninsular born Spaniards from the entire land. The effect in Sonora was to reduce the missionary force to two friars: Raphael Díaz, a Spaniard with friends in Arispe, and Mexican born José Pérez Llera. What an incredible task for two! Pérez Llera remained at San Ignacio from which he administered all of the western desert missions— Tubutama, Oquitoa, Caborca and all their visitas. The chain of missions along the northern route fell to Díaz who roved from Cocóspera to San Xavier del Bac, including the presidios at Tubac, Tucson, and Terrenate. The Mexican law of secularization had the same effect on the missions as the Jesuit expulsion in 1767 because all the properties were confiscated by civil administrators. The two friars were bereft of all power and monies, and thus the Indians were deprived of their help. It was a sad situation for the native population. Although some of the properties were returned in 1830, the essential damage had been done and it was only a matter of time before the powerful miitary leaders of the north interpreted the laws in their own favor. The lands quickly fell into the hands of a very few families—a social phenomenon that has plagued Mexico for centuries.

Father Pérez Llera acted as mission president until 1837. He succeeded in doubling the missionary force from two to four. But the team of friars were old and powerless. By 1836 the assigned missioners had grown to six, yet these lasted only a few more years because Pérez Llera left the Pimería in 1837 as the winds of political change shifted once again in Mexico. The others either abandoned their impossible situations or died. By 1841 there were only two left once again. It was the beginning of the absolute end of the missions that were once so proud under Padre Kino.

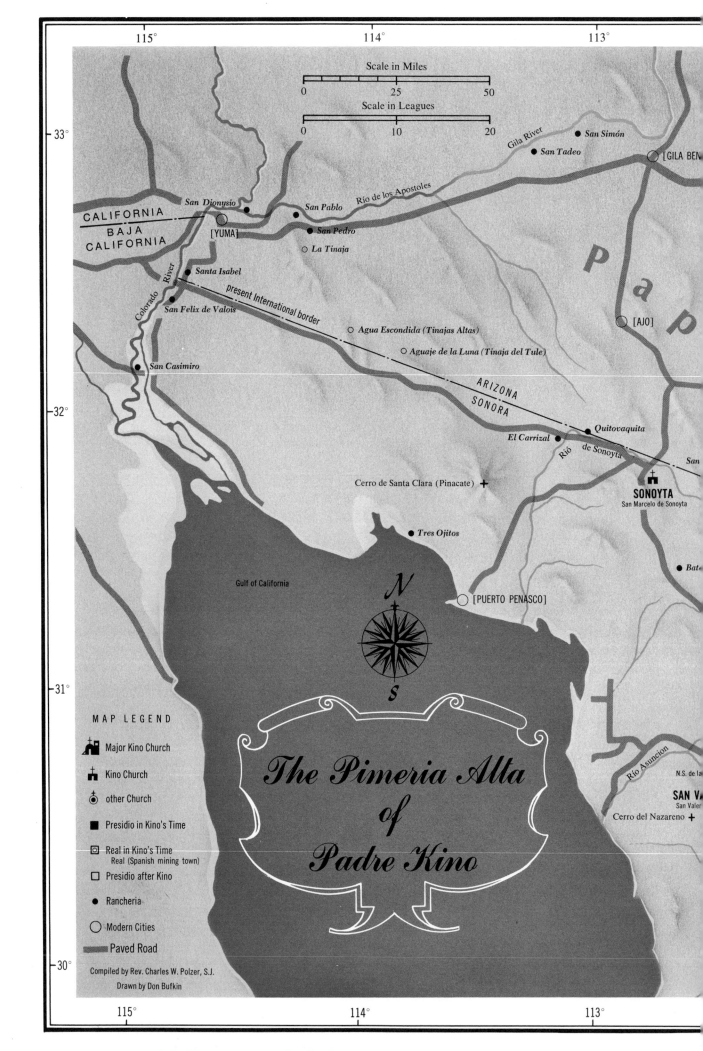

The Pimeria Alta
of
Padre Kino

MAP LEGEND

- Major Kino Church
- Kino Church
- other Church
- Presidio in Kino's Time
- Real in Kino's Time
  Real (Spanish mining town)
- Presidio after Kino
- Rancheria
- Modern Cities
- Paved Road

Compiled by Rev. Charles W. Polzer, S.J.
Drawn by Don Bufkin

Scale in Miles
0   25   50

Scale in Leagues
0   10   20

115°   114°   113°

33°

32°

31°

30°

Gila River
● San Simón
● San Tadeo
○ [GILA BEN

San Dionysio ●
San Pablo ●
Río de los Apostoles
San Pedro ●
○ La Tinaja

CALIFORNIA
BAJA
CALIFORNIA
[YUMA]

P a p

Santa Isabel ●
San Felix de Valois ●
present International border
○ [AJO]

Colorado River

○ Agua Escondida (Tinajas Altas)
○ Aguaje de la Luna (Tinaja del Tule)

● San Casimiro

ARIZONA
SONORA

El Carrizal ●
● Quitovaquita
Río de Sonoyta
San

Cerro de Santa Clara (Pinacate) +

SONOYTA
San Marcelo de Sonoyta

● Tres Ojitos

Gulf of California

● Bat

○ [PUERTO PENASCO]

N
S

Río Asuncion
N.S. de la

SAN V
San Valer
Cerro del Nazareno

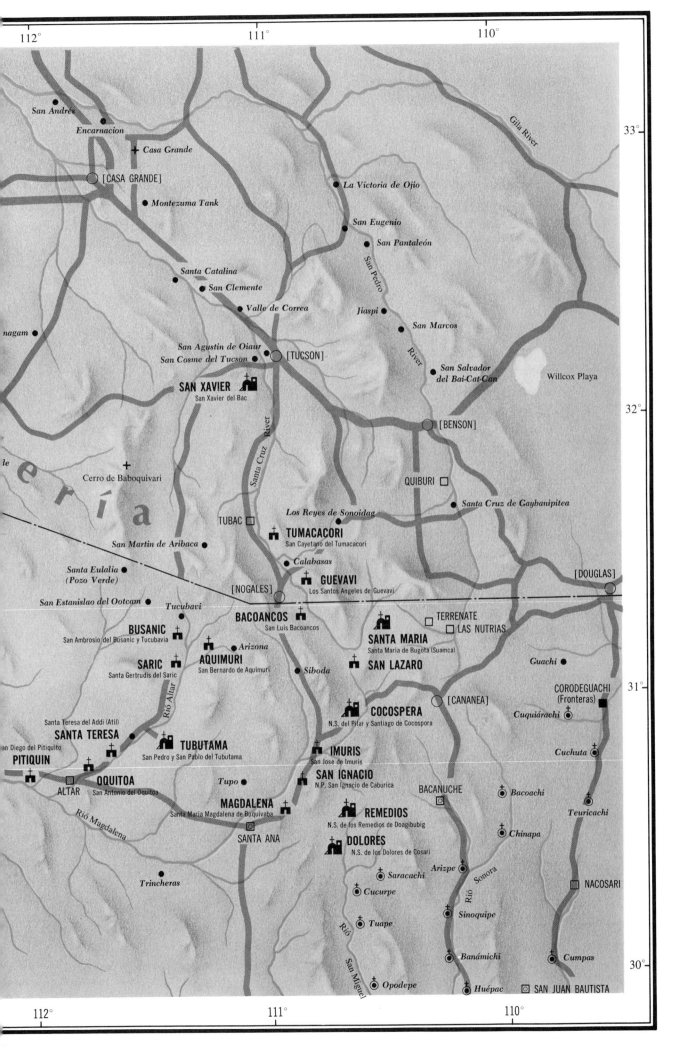

112° 111° 110°

33°

San Andrés
Encarnación
+ Casa Grande
◉ [CASA GRANDE]
● Montezuma Tank
La Victoria de Ojio ●
San Eugenio ●
San Pantaleón ●
Santa Catalina ●
● San Clemente
● Valle de Correa
Jiaspi ●
San Marcos ●
nagam ●
San Pedro
River
San Agustin de Oiaur ●
San Cosme del Tucson ● ◉ [TUCSON]
San Salvador
del Bai-Cat-Can ●
Willcox Playa
⛪ SAN XAVIER
San Xavier del Bac

32°

◉ [BENSON]
e r í a
+ Cerro de Baboquivari
Santa Cruz River
QUIBURI □
le
Santa Cruz de Gaybanipitea ●
TUBAC □
Los Reyes de Sonoidag ●
San Martin de Aribaca ●
⛪ TUMACACORI
San Cayetano del Tumacacori
[DOUGLAS] ◉
Santa Eulalia
(Pozo Verde) ●
● Calabasas
⛪ GUEVAVI
Los Santos Angeles de Guevavi
San Estanislao del Ootcam ●
Tucubavi ●
TERRENATE □
□ LAS NUTRIAS
BACOANCOS ⛪
San Luis Bacoancos
⛪ BUSANIC
San Ambrosio del Busanic y Tucubavia
⛪ AQUIMURI
● Arizona
San Bernardo de Aquimuri
⛪ SANTA MARIA
Santa Maria de Bugota (Suamca)
Guachi ●
⛪ SARIC
Santa Gertrudis del Saric
● Siboda
⛪ SAN LAZARO

31°

Rió Altar
⛪ COCOSPERA
N.S. del Pilar y Santiago de Cocospora
[CANANEA] □
CORODEGUACHI
(Fronteras) ■
Cuquiárachi ⛪◉
Santa Teresa del Addi (Atil)
⛪ SANTA TERESA ●
⛪ TUBUTAMA
San Pedro y San Pablo del Tubutama
⛪ IMURIS
San Jose de Imuris
Cuchuta ⛪◉
San Diego del Pitiquito
⛪ PITIQUIN
⛪ SAN IGNACIO
N.P. San Ignacio de Caburica
BACANUCHE ◉
⛪ OQUITOA
● Tupo
Bacoachi ⛪◉
Teuricachi ⛪◉
ALTAR □ San Antonio del Oquitoa
⛪ MAGDALENA
Santa Maria Magdalena de Buquivaba
⛪ REMEDIOS
N.S. de los Remedios de Doagibubig
Chinapa ⛪◉
Rió Magdalena
SANTA ANA
⛪ DOLORES
N.S. de los Dolores de Cosari
● Trincheras
Arizpe ⛪◉
Rió Sonora
NACOSARI □
Saracachi ⛪◉
Cucurpe ⛪◉
Sinoquipe ⛪◉
Rió San Miguel
Tuape ⛪◉
Banámichi ⛪◉
Cumpas ⛪◉

30°

Opodepe ⛪◉
Huépac ⛪◉
□ SAN JUAN BAUTISTA

112° 111° 110°

THE MISSIONS OF PADRE KINO

Contemporary Americans seldom question their stereotyped concepts of the "Spanish mission." Some concepts are pious ones—of devoted religious, obedient neophytes, and quaint churches in the wilderness. Some are impious —of domineering clerics, enslaved natives, and fortress compounds. How does the historian disabuse anyone of these commonly held ideas that have sprouted in the darkness of ignorance? The task of history is to enlighten the past so that present and future generations can know the genuine contributions our predecessors have made.

Although we speak of the Spanish mission or the mission system, in reality each mission recorded a distinct, even diverse, history. The networks of missions in different regions and in different epochs may have been analogous, but they were certainly not the same. In northern New Spain (Mexico) five or six systems can be described. The Kino mission chain was only a part of one of them.

The first two, and earliest, systems were formed along the spine of the Sierra Madre Occidental. In the late 16th century Franciscan friars opened mission centers among the Chichimec tribes while the Jesuit blackrobes were invited to labor along the Pacific slope. Franciscan evangelization in the central plateau occasioned their entry into New Mexico where the Spaniards encountered the highly organized Pueblo societies. By contrast the Jesuit missionaries more commonly dealt with scattered nations in the rugged mountains and river valleys. In the early 18th century the Jesuits opened a new chain of missions in Baja California that required significantly innovative procedures for administration and supply. At the same time the Franciscans pressed eastward into Texas where their missions played a dual role in conversion and frontier defense. When the missions of Alta California were established in the late 18th century, the role of the mission had undergone substantial modification due to the secular goals of military security and overland supply. Nowhere at any time was there a uniform mission system.

Unfortunately too many writers have created romantic fictions about mission life. Typically, a stalwart, rugged man of God rides into the desert wilderness and with bare hands builds a monumental church on an idyllic hilltop. Curious natives respond to reverberating bells; songs fill the air; and fields of grain wave in the golden sun. The truth, however, was quite different. Usually the new missionary rode into long-established native villages under military escort; negotiations ensued in which the Indians decided to accept or decline the invitation to have a European living and working among them. Only after long years of patient ministry was a missionary able to penetrate new frontiers and find new peoples who might be eager to accept him and the Faith. It was almost exclusively a matter of the missionary's established reputation.

Missions were also successful to the extent that the initial enticements of food, clothing, and supplies expanded into richer benefits of education and incorporation into the comparative opulence of Spanish society. Indeed, the Spaniard saw the mission as a means of acculturating and pacifying fiercely independent peoples. The religious considered the mission as the only reliable stepping stone to salvation. The Indian saw the mission as a tolerable, if threatening, means to enter a new way of life. In other words, the mission was a complex social reality that served multiple purposes and was perceived according to very different scales of value.

Some generalizations about Spanish missions are valid. In the case of the Jesuit missions there was a relatively consistent plan of organization and administration. New Spain constituted a "province" which came under the jurisdiction of a single superior or "Provincial." Every member of the Society in New Spain was subject to his authority. For reasons of administrative, as well as religious asceticism, an individual Jesuit also answered to a local superior or "Rector." Interposed between the provincial and the Rector frequently was a "Visitor" who held limited, delegated powers from the Provincial; this bridged the geographic gap between Mexico City and the far flung frontiers. Contrary to popular opinion a missionary 2000 kilometers from Mexico City was not free to act independently. Even expeditions into neighboring lands required prior, explicit permission from the Provincial or the Visitor. Hence the chain of command in the Jesuit missions began with the missionary on the frontier who answered to the local Rector; the Rector, to the Visitor, and through the Visitor to the Provincial; the Provincial answered directly to the General of the Society in Rome.

The entire missionary sector was divided into "rectorates" that were responsible for clusters of missions. A particular mission often consisted of a "cabecera" or resident headquarters and several near-by "visitas" or mission stations—the distinction normally being in the residency status of a missionary. A rectorate, in turn, comprised several cabeceras. In this way the whole of northwestern New Spain's Jesuit missions were organized.

When Padre Kino came to the northwestern frontier of New Spain in 1687, he was building on the reputation and hard work of a half century of predecessors. His Blackrobe companions chose the site of Cosari for the new cabecera among the Pimas Altos. This new conversion was nothing more than the next stage in a long-standing plan of mission expansion. Kino did not ride in alone on horseback and dazzle the natives with linguistic prowess or magic. He rode in with well known missionaries who introduced him to the Indians, now eager to have their own resident European because they recognized from afar how the other villages had fared under Spanish dominion.

Padre Kino named his new post Nuestra Señora de los Dolores de Cosari. Although the initial name stood for only an individual mission station, it almost immediately became the cabecera of a series of small visitas, such as San Ignacio and Remedios. As acceptance of the missionary program spread rapidly through the Pimería Alta, Kino established new cabecceras where other Jesuits became the resident missionaries; Dolores soon advanced to the status of a rectorate with Padre Kino as the first local superior. And in this sense we moderns look back at the whole of the Pimería Alta and call the twenty-odd missions of the rectorate of Dolores the missions of Padre Kino. He had something to do with all of them; he was remotely in charge of all of them; but, there were several other Jesuit missionaries immediately responsible for their care and development.

When Padre Kino rode the Indian trails at the turn of the 18th century, he selected many existent villages as sites for future missions. On the following pages several of these sites are described in word and picture. None of the imposing Spanish colonial churches still standing today, however, were the handiwork of Padre Kino himself. The splendid buildings at San Xavier del Bac, Caborca and Tubutama represent the last flourish of Franciscan efforts in a land they inherited from the expelled Jesuits. All of these churches were erected nearly a century after Kino had established the first missions in these widespread pueblos.

Less than a quarter century after Kino's death most of the proud structures he had personally built with his team of skilled craftsmen were crumbling into ruin. Twenty years of scarce manpower and neglect brought the churches to the brink of total collapse. When a new wave of missionary replacements arrived in the 1730s they each felt as though they had to begin again. And even their churches, constructed through the middle of the century have—for the most part—all disappeared or given way to newer, sturdier structures. It is all part of the saga of growth—of death and resurrection.

Actually all that remains of the personal work of Padro Kino are a few deeply protected adobes inside the walls of Cocóspera and under the mounded ruins of Dolores and Remedios. Kino's own churches were proud buildings constructed by Indian craftsmen under his continual supervision. Now they are only sad monuments to the ravages of weather, Indian wars, revolutions, and blindly ignorant treasure hunters. The little physical trace that remains today of Padre Kino's presence will soon disappear as each year the summer rains cleanse the savage wounds of metal detectors and shovels that have surpassed the frenzied destruction of mission sites by Apaches and senseless revolutionaries. But even the inexorable forces of change and decay will never touch the persistent memory of Kino and the men who catapulted this desert into the annals of history. Whether a humble Jesuit ruin or a magnificent Franciscan monument, the sites and churches of the Pimería Alta will always be the missions of Padre Kino who propelled them into history.

To the person who takes the time to visit the missions of northern Sonora and Arizona will come the realization that the finest hours of life are spent in helping those in need. These great mission churches rose up in the desert because people had learned the value of cooperation, sacrifice, and dignity. If these missions continue to fall into ruin, the tragedy will not be the loss of the buildings, but the loss of the sense of human solidarity that men like Kino developed in the desert southwest.

NUESTRA SEÑORA de los DOLORES

Dolores, mother mission of the Pimería Alta, was founded on March 13, 1687, when Padre Eusebio Kino decided to base his apostolic ministries at the Pima village of Cosari. The site of Dolores was a favorite ranchería among the Pimas and under the guidance of skillful missionaries it promised to yield even greater returns. Although the first mission buildings were temporary, by 1693 there was a "good and roomy church with seven bells, well provided with vestments, linens, and altars; a water-powered mill, a carpentry shop, blacksmith shop, herds of cattle and oxen, horses, a farm, orchards, vineyards, and a winery."

Despite this prolific effort Kino's interest and familiarity with other regions of the Pimería deterred him from making Dolores too permanent a headquarters. His major efforts at construction were focused on more remote sites along the frontier, such as Caborca and Bac. Dolores was destined to return to the dust. Only ten years after Kino's death Jesuit reports speak of Dolores as unhealthful, humid, and cold; the church was falling to the ground.

Many Indians had moved away and during the ensuing decade many of those who stayed died in recurrent epidemics. By 1732 the mission was all but abandoned; too few people were living there to warrant restoration. Padre Duquesney noted in 1744 that the mission had been vacated.

The population of the San Miguel and Cocóspera river valleys had declined so far by 1748 that Padre Ignacio Keller consolidated the survivors at Cocóspera where he could serve them from his own station at Santa María Suamca. The decline moved so rapidly that Dolores was only partly inhabited by 1750, formally abandoned in 1762, and defunct, for all intents and purposes, by 1763.

Wandering Spanish colonials settled in the mission ruins during the later Jesuit period. They converted some of its buildings to new uses and by the time the Pimería Alta came into the hands of the Franciscans, the buildings and lands had been made into a hacienda.

All that remains of Dolores today is the magnificent setting and some flattened mounds to remind us of the glory that has vanished from the Sorrowful Mother of the Pimería Alta.

NUESTRA SEÑORA de los REMEDIOS

Remedios, of all Kino's missions, was the reluctant one. No sooner had Padre Kino visited the village of Coágibubig than the Pimas living there reneged on their acceptance of building a mission. But the padre's persuasive powers won out and within seven years a large church and living quarters were under construction. The mission compound rose in slow agony; the records continually refer to the church and quarters at Remedios as "nearly completed" for four more years.

By 1699 the walls were up and the roofing was to be begun, but torrential rains flooded the apse, soaked the

adobe foundations and washed out the presbytery. The damage was repaired and in a few months the small church was useable. No sooner were these initial structures completed than Kino commenced work on two large and spacious churches, here at Remedios and at Cocóspera. Both churches reached completion at the same time and Padre Kino planned a whole week of celebrations to dedicate the two churches in January, 1704. With a few minor exceptions they were architectural reflections of one another. "Each church has a high cupola set on the arches of the two chapels which form the transept, and each cupola has a sightly lantern above and in the middle."

Unfortunately, both missions were built within range of frequent Apache raiding. Defense towers were added to the churches but this did not deter the enemy from destructive attacks. After Kino's time the pueblo of Remedios dwindled in size and importance. Epidemics took their toll along with Apache arrows. The church was crumbling in 1723, in ruins by 1730, and totally abandoned before 1740. Unlike Dolores over the rise to the south, Remedios never even became spoils for a future hacienda — everything of importance was gone. Even the vestments and church ornaments were transferred to Santa María Suamca for safe-keeping while a new mission was prepared among the Sobaípuris in the north.

Remedios is but a memory and a name which belongs to the hills surrounding it. The splendor of its church lives on only in the decimated ruins of Cocóspera, its twin in construction and its survivor through time.

NUESTRA SEÑORA del PILAR y SANTIAGO de COCOSPERA

No church in northern Sonora has ever held the same degree of fascination created by the lonely ruin of Cocóspera. Situated on a high bluff above the picturesque Cocóspera valley, this mission has witnessed the rise and fall of empire. Apaches used the valley as a natural route of attack on the central Pimería. The Spanish used the region as a natural staging area for defensive forays along the frontier and as a jumping off place for explorations. Its rich river lands provided the colonial residents with abundant produce, and they in turn offered the numerous services and skills so precious to frontier life from the pueblo which grew up around the mission. After the collapse of Spanish imperial power the deserted mission-town became the home for remnants of French and American adventurers whose invasions of Sonora during the turbulent 1800's failed.

The original church was the near twin of Remedios mission. Padre Kino laid the foundations for a large church with transepts and adobe arches. The inner walls of the ruin show clearly that the Franciscans built their church around the ruined shell of the Jesuit mission so frequently ravaged by Apache attacks. The facade of the Kino church was flanked by large, square defense towers which later formed the bases for twin bell towers. The windows and doors were constructed of posts and lintels with flat surfaced splays and wood-grill apertures. The interior walls were coated with a thin white plaster and decorated by red ocher paintings.

When the Franciscans renovated the mission in the late eighteenth century, they lined the adobe shell with fired bricks, raised strong rock buttresses outside the nave, and erected a new brick and stucco facade. The church interior was faced with brick and heavily plastered thus permitting an exuberance of raised plaster reliefs incorporating a variety of swags, urns, and scallop shells.

The mission ruin of Cocóspera is easily reached today by taking the highway from Imuris to Cananea. The site is located on the northwest side of the road. Perhaps it is too accessible because it has been continually ravaged by misguided treasure hunters whose pick-hammers and shovels have almost destroyed this monument to man and God on the desert frontier.

SAN IGNACIO de CABURICA

San Ignacio de Caburica, six miles up river from Magdalena de Kino, rests peacefully near some low hills around which the river veers on its course from Imuris. San Ignacio is one of the true delights of the Sonoran mission frontier. In modern times the mission and village have been all but forgotten in the rush of business and travel.

The mission site was chosen by Padre Kino in 1687 because Caburica was a populous Indian ranchería. A series of small chapels served as visitas or as temporary buildings until 1693 when Padre Agustín de Campos arrived to transform Caburica into a cabecera. His new church was burned during the Pima uprising of 1695, but soon rebuilt. For forty-three years San Ignacio served as the headquarters for Padre Campos, one of the longest terms of missionary service on record in the Pimería Alta. Quite understandably San Ignacio captured Campos' heart because of its central location and agreeable climate.

Campos' longevity and missionary skills made San Ignacio a training ground for new Jesuits moving into the missions of the Pimería. Highly skilled in the various Piman dialects, Campos' presence at San Ignacio naturally turned it into a language school and proving ground for those who would be assigned to other more distant churches. After Campos left in 1736 Padre Gaspar Stiger filled the same role of teacher and superior until his death in 1762.

Although the rector of the missions did not always reside at San Ignacio, the Pimería Alta was effectively administered from this location throughout the post-Kino period, or roughly until the expulsion of the Jesuits in 1767. The early years of Franciscan administration were dominated by the centrality of this mission, but as westward expansion overtook the Pimería, San Ignacio deferred to the more northerly and westerly missions of San Xavier del Bac, San Pedro y Pablo del Tubutama and La Concepción de Caborca. When the whole northern frontier was consolidated into the diocese of Sonora San Ignacio drifted into oblivion. Today the pueblo is a jewel of placidity.

No thorough investigation of San Ignacio has ever been carried out, but evidence indicates that the present church is reminiscent of the architecture employed by the Jesuits in the Pimería. Padre Stiger built a completely new church here in 1753 and church records imply that this structure was merely renovated and remodelled in subsequent years. Both Franciscan and secular priests undertook extensive remodelling, but comparative study shows that the bell tower, size of the nave, and the circular mesquite-log staircase were characteristic of the earlier churches of the Pimería.

SAN PEDRO y SAN PABLO del TUBUTAMA

A visit to Tubutama is to relive the missionary past—but without missionaries. Although the pueblo is well off the main highway, it is accessible by paved roads. From any angle of approach the town looms up like a welcome oasis in the desert, dominated by the squared towers of a white mission church. The church fronts on a plaza that is frequently void of cars or trucks; usually one or two horses stand in the shade of local cantinas. A pervading silence is broken occasionally by the voices of children at play or by a burro train clopping through the streets.

In 1687 Padre Kino was invited to Tubutama. Immediately he began construction on a small church and mission visita. The struggling new mission was the scene of the outbreak of the Pima rebellion of 1695. The mission itself was burned out and the crops destroyed. But it was only a short while before the repentant Indians repaired the damage and Tubutama took its quiet place in the history of the Pimería. As isolated as the town now seems, Tubutama served as the jumping off station for the bold crossings of the Papaguería that had to be undertaken to explore the western deserts.

After Kino's time manpower was at a premium and Tubutama was maintained only as a mission visita. By 1730, however, more men were sent as missionaries into the Pimería and Tubutama was raised to the level of a cabecera at which time a new church was erected. Padre Jacob Sedelmayr, another famous Jesuit explorer, built a church here at mid-century. But it came to grief during the 1751 Pima rebellion when Luis of Sáric burned the church and murdered several residents of the pueblo. Once the rebellion was quelled the church was again rebuilt; a decent structure was reported here by Padre Manuel Aguirre in 1764.

When the Franciscans took over in 1768, the mission enjoyed a favored place in the Pimería and a new, more elaborate church was built here in 1788. This is the same structure that graces the pueblo today. Recent repair and restoration have paid strict attention to the earliest known details so that the church today remains a fine example of what it once was. The older mission buildings were apparently closer to the river bluff than the present church, but all trace of them has disappeared. In the early 1950s a group of American adventurers, searching for the fictitious Jesuit treasure, nearly dynamited the pueblo. Fortunately the men were stopped in time or another masterpiece of colonial architecture would have crumbled in tragic ruin.

Another stunning change at Tubutama was the construction of Cuatemoc Resevoir, damming up the ever flowing Altar River where mission fields once flowered.

SAN ANTONIO DEL OQUITOA

Arriving in Altar one never gets the impression it was at the junction of two major Sonoran rivers. Irrigation projects and deep water wells have so altered the flow of water that only a wary traveler would suspect how the terrain looked in colonial times. The nearest village up river from Altar is the quaint community of San Antonio del Oquitoa. A simple, lonely church surmounts a rounded hill above the town; its stark lines are surrounded by a sun-seared cemetery.

Oquitoa was never an important historical site even in Padre Kino's day. What fame it had was infamous because residents of this town were the murderers of Padre Saeta in Caborca. But now Oquitoa has taken its quiet place in history and has become a favored spot along the Kino mission trail.

In 1980 restoration work was completed on the then decaying church. Fascinating discoveries were made of earlier construction techniques and decorative details. Now San Antonio del Oquitoa has taken a position of pride in the history of Sonora. The narrow nave, thick adobe walls, and beam ceiling remain as one of the last vestiges of a truly bygone era. Oquitoa doesn't seem very different today from what it must have been in the 18th century.

Rarely in Jesuit mission country does one encounter a church under the patronage of Franciscan saints. In the case of San Antonio del Oquitoa it appears that the patron of the village was chosen because the first resident priest in the altar valley was Padre Antonio Arias at Tubutama. Soon after his appointment Oquitoa became a visita under his care. It is curious how strongly history is written in the traces of unassuming names.

SAN DIEGO del PITIQUITO

In the days of Padre Kino, Pitiquito was never a very important pueblo although he frequently visited there. For years it remained a dependent mission station of Caborca. In 1772 Fray Antonio de los Reyes, later the first bishop of Arispe, reported that there was no church at the site. The Franciscans began the present structure in 1778; since then, the church has undergone extensive modification.

The history of Pitiquito has been vague at best. In the early months of 1967 the residents of the town became terrified at what they thought were the appearances of spirits in the church. Skeletons, eyes, hands, and words emerged and vanished on the massive white-washed walls throughout the interior of the church. The more timorous

people interpreted these words and figures as omens predicting the immediate end of the world.

But on investigaiton it was found that the ladies of the town had been cleaning the church for a fiesta. They used detergents to wash the walls. And a day or so after each cleansing figures and words would appear on the surface. What no one knew is that the whole church had been decorated with large liturgical and doctrinal murals, but the paintings are so old that not even the oldest resident has the faintest recollection of ever seeing the church with anything but a white-washed interior. A request has been made to the Mexican federal government to attempt to restore the murals since they could well become the best example of catechetical art known for this period of Sonoran history.

LA PURÍSIMA CONCEPCION
de NUESTRA SEÑORA de CABORCA

Deceptively peaceful, Caborca rises along the banks of the Río Concepción at the heart of an amazingly fertile plain in the great western desert of Sonora. Padre Kino himself was impressed by its potential and began constructing a new mission here in 1693. He entrusted his hopes for the mission's future to Padre Francisco Xavier Saeta, but the Pima rebellion of 1695 demolished those hopes with the murder of Saeta and the pillaging of the village. Caborca, however, recovered and for a half century grew in importance as the western staging area for explorations into the Colorado delta.

But Caborca's calm was shattered again in the Pima rebellion of 1751; this time the blood of Padre Tomás Tello stained the sands of the agricultural heartland. Again peace returned to the broad valley and the agricultural economy pulsed with new importance. Although one might suspect that such an isolated place would eventually experience peace, it did not; violence broke out in 1857 when Henry A. Crabb and his filibuster army be-

sieged the townspeople in the mission church. His ill-fated attempt to seize northern Sonora ended in the execution of his entire force on the mission steps. Residents claim that the bullet marks on the facade date from this historical episode.

The present church was built between 1803 and 1809. It shows many architectural similarities to San Xavier del Bac. A large convento once stood to the north of the church but raging floods in the early 20th century ripped into this construction and also eroded away the sacristy and rear of the sanctuary. The Mexican government has since restored the church and made it a national monument. Caborca is less remembered for being an important mission and the scene of two martyrdoms than for its being the place where American expansion into Mexico was halted by the bullets of patriots.

A new plaza was created in front of the church in 1967. The small archway which serves as the formal entrance to the plaza was made from the stone facade of an ancient chapel in the town of Batuc which has been inundated by the waters of El Novillo dam on the Río Yaqui.

SAN CAYETANO del TUMACACORI

Tumacácori's past is elusive. All the maps of Padre Kino indicate an Indian village of Tumacácori on the east bank of the Santa Cruz River. Apparently the site was a convenient crossing place where the waters of the river had a chance to broaden out. From Tumacácori the trail crossed the river to the west and continued on down to San Xavier del Bac. Actually the Pima settlement of Tumacácori gained importance only after the establishment of the presidio of Tubac in 1752. Prior to this the main concentration of Indians was at Los Angeles de Guevavi, an extensive mission some twelve miles up river. In many ways the early history of Tumacácori is the history of Guevavi. Guevavi, like Tumacácori, was an original Kino visita, but a major mission complex was not built here until after Kino's time, in 1732 when Padre Johann Gazhofer took charge.

Exactly ten miles south of Tumacácori was also located the mission visita of Calabasas. Throughout Jesuit times there was nothing more here than a small wayside chapel, and its importance varied with the shifts in Indian population. It seems that because of recurrent Apache raids the Sobaípuris pulled out of the San Pedro river valley and took refuge at these missions within the sphere of Spanish protection.

Since the present mission bears a new name, San José de Tumacácori, it is most probable that the church was erected on a new and somewhat different site from that of Kino's. This mission was erected in 1773 and rebuilt at various times. Construction was suspended in 1822 due to the lack of funds although the church remained in use until secularization became effective in the 1840's.

LOS SANTOS ANGELES DE GUEVAVI

Situated on the Guevavi Ranch on the east bank of the Río Santa Cruz are the last traces of Arizona's oldest Jesuit mission, Los Santos Angeles de Guevavi. The site was selected by Padre Kino in the early 1690s because of its centrality to the scattered rancherías of the upper river valley. Through the first years of its existence it was known variously as San Raphael Archangel, San Gabriel Archangel and finally as Los Santos Angeles; no one could remember which patron was foremost anymore. Its first resident missionary was Padre Juan de San Martín who arrived in 1701; but the mission was soon abandoned and not until 1732 did Guevavi again host a resident priest.

Although reconstructed after the ravages of the 1751 Pima rebellion, Guevavi's fortunes waned and by the last quarter of the 18th century it was reduced to a visita—often exposed to Apache raids and too far from protection by the garrison at Tubac.

THE VISITAS OF THE SAN PEDRO, SANTA MARIA AND ALTAR RIVERS

Curiously the most scenic sections of the Sonoran border are rarely seen by tourists or even residents of the region. The natural causeways of communication in colonial times were the river valleys that are avoided by techniques of modern transportation. Hence the splendors known so well to the men who made history in the Pimería Alta are enigmas to us moderns who have come so suddenly on the complex past.

The lower reaches of the Río San Pedro were studded with short-lived rancherías and potential visitas. The Apache menace drove the Sobaipuri Pimas from their traditional homes and eliminated the potential for conversion. The upper parts of the Río Santa María (the older name for the Río Santa Cruz) boasted a cabecera at Santa María Suamca and visitas at San Lázaro and San Luis Bacoancos. But a furious attack in 1768 obliterated the village and mission at Suamca. The weakened condition of the Opata-Sobaipuri villages contributed to the collapse of the defensive perimeter along the Pimería Alta. The over exposed and under staffed garrisons at Terrenate, Tubac and Altar were never able to hold the frontier with safety.

The visitas along the Altar River present a similar history. Some of the visitas along this reliable water course rose to full mission status only to fall back again into ruin and abandonment. A case in point is San Francisco Ati, or Atil or Adid. Whatever the proprieties of the name, the place was made famous by Padre Ignaz Pfefferkorn in his classic *Description of Sonora*. When Pfefferkorn worked there in 1756, traces of the Kino chapel were still there because the place had been bypassed in the rebellion of '51. Ati fell on hard times after Pfefferkorn was transferred to Cucurpe. Apaches raided it frequently, missionaries refused to minister to its flock, and eventually the vestments and church furnishings were lost or unuseable.

Farther up the Río Altar is the important town of Sáric that also rose to mission status for a short while. Now the people of the town can only dispute where the mission might have been because its last vestiges have been so badly mistreated and forgotten. The same story goes for Tucubavia, Busanic, and other ephemeral villages along the ancient riverway.

SAN XAVIER del BAC

The foundations for the great mission of San Xavier del Bac were laid in 1700 by Padre Eusebio Kino. Some years before he had been impressed by this largest of the Pima villages along the Santa Cruz. But even after the mission was completed, it remained vacant throughout the first decades of the 18th century. The first resident missionary to remain longer than a year was Padre José Torres Perea who arrived in 1740.

The Kino church was apparently destroyed in whole or in part because the church used by Padre Philip Ségesser was replaced by another that was extensively damaged in the rebellion of 1751. A third, or perhaps fourth church, was built here by Padre Alonso Espinosa in 1762. This large adobe structure was the same one utilized by the Franciscans when they took over the mission in 1768. This large church was located west of the present magnificent mission, begun in 1783 and completed in 1797. Hence the present church does not date back to the Jesuit period although the site does. Archaeological investigations in 1967 disclosed the location of an earlier church which was later destroyed by new construction, but the location of the Kino church remains a mystery.

Bac's history has always been fascinating because it has always housed the largest Indian populations. For centuries it has been the meeting place and training ground for the *hechiceros,* medicine men, of neighboring tribes. From here Kino sent out messengers to learn about the peculiar blue shells which figured so prominently in the discovery that California was not an island. It was Kino's dream to move his headquarters to Bac, but the lack of men to assume responsibilities at Dolores made the move impossible.

Today mission San Xavier del Bac is one of the colonial art treasures of America. Its baroque architecture is a monument to the splendor of the civilization that first came to the desert frontier of Sonora and Arizona. Surrounded by fields of grain and cotton and by the adobe dwellings of the Pápagos, it is a page from the past that has been forgotten in the haste of freeways and the waste of crowded cities.

The MISSIONS of the LOWER GILA and COLORADO RIVERS

The Indian pueblos along the Gila bore a litany of apostolic names but to call them missions is to raise them to a dignity beyond the reality. At most, they were visitas for the missionaries of San Xavier del Bac, San Pedro del Tubutama, Santa María Suamca, and Los Angeles de Guevavi. Yet they have been traditionally so de-emphasized that their existence as visitas has been overlooked.

From the time of Padre Kino these pueblos were considered as potential missions and were to be visited whenever possible. Mission maps for the entire first half-century in the 1700's depict the chain of villages. There was continual contact, first with Kino, then Campos, and down through the years by Padres Ignacio Keller, Jacob Sedelmayr, and quite probably Gaspar Stiger and Alonso Espinosa. They were certainly attended by the Franciscans, most notably Fray Francisco Garcés.

It is nearly impossible to imagine the meaning of the Gila and Colorado missions today. The villages and their Indian populations have long since disappeared just as the shallow-draft steamers that once plied the desert river waters. But in the days of the active missions of the Pimería they were outposts on a frontier that strained toward California, the last havens of supply for the men who were penetrating the "Moqui" lands to the north and west.

The central pueblo along this coveted chain was San Dionisio, roughly identifiable with present day Yuma. The melodious Christian names of villages that ran upstream from San Dionisio are gone; San Pedro and Pablo, San Thadeo and San Simón have given way to Dome and Wellton. Thus the modern American frontier has erased any memory of these ancient sites where the Gila Pimas and Cocomaricopas met the Cross and Crown.

The shorter chain of missions down the Colorado among the Yuman peoples bore the names of the patrons of Spanish royalty — Santa Isabel, San Félix de Valois, San Casimiro. But none of these pueblos reached any significant level of development until long after the Jesuit expulsion in 1767. In the last quarter of the eighteenth century the misguided policies of Teodoro de Croix, the governor of the northern provinces, spelled an end to the missionary hopes enkindled here by Padre Kino.

De Croix's policies were a direct attack on the mission system. He wanted instant integration which amounted to sudden slavery for the Indians along the Colorado. Fray Francisco Garcés, O.F.M., tried valiantly to continue the expansion of the missions, but his policies crumpled under the "enlightened" guidance of De Croix. The Indians of the Colorado saw clearly through the Spanish colonial plan for them. So they rose in revolt in July, 1781, massacring some fifty Spaniards including Fray Garcés and Captain Fernando Rivera y Moncada.

The Jesuit visitas along the Colorado by then had disappeared with the shift of Indian population centers, and the Franciscan missions were now burned to the ground. The Yuman nation maintained stiff resistance to Spanish conquest and the mission system never revived in the river delta.

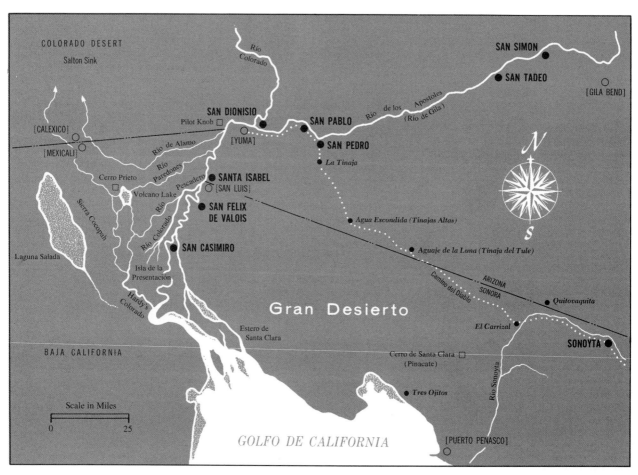

THE MISSIONS AS OTHERS SAW THEM

by Thomas H. Naylor

The buildings that today comprise the "Kino chain of missions" stand witness to the inexorable forces of time. Whether from neglect or abandonment to the harsh physical forces of the Sonoran Desert, or due to a royal decision from Madrid to exile and replace an entire religious order with another, the churches have undergone rebuilding and continual change. While some of the monuments have slowly eroded back into the earth, most of the buildings have seen periods of reconstruction and remodeling—right up to the present day.

Each church is unique as to its community setting, particular history and the amount of interest and concern it has been shown. Lacking a protective community to care for it, Cocóspera has been ravaged by man and the elements to a near formless ruin. Only very recently has it been given any protection. Other Pimería churches have succumbed entirely. San Ignacio, Oquitoa and Tubutama have always enjoyed the care and protection of the small but immensely proud villages nestled at their feet. Shunted aside in the wake of the agro-boom, Caborca's mission church nearly fell total victim to flood erosion. Rescued because of its nationalistic importance as the scene of a Mexican victory over invading *norteamericanos,* the lost sections have now been rebuilt; the restored church and *con-vento* appear on the way to becoming a museum. San Xavier del Bac found itself in the United States after 1853. That fact, and its proximity to heavily traveled routes and to Tucson, placed it in the limelight, and a succession of church funded projects and state and federal assistance has beautifully preserved it. Being the finest example of Spanish colonial architecture in the U.S. has not hurt San Xavier either. Tumacácori and Guevavi, also in Arizona, have fared much worse. Considerably less impressive and already in varying states of ruin, Tumacácori was eventually saved from oblivion by the National Park Service, but only mounds and fragments of walls mark the site of Guevavi today.

The visual record of the Pimería churches begins in the middle of the 19th century in the form of drawings and sketches. Among the best are those of J. Ross Browne in 1864 and Alphonse Pinart in 1879, examples of which appear in the following pages. The earliest photographs date from the 1870s and are relatively plentiful after 1900. Their quality and condition vary considerably. In the views that follow every attempt was made to include those that were most skillfully made and which most dramatically document the ever-changing churches through time.

SAN XAVIER

Taken probably in 1881, this view by H. T. Watkins shows the mortuary chapel wall intact and only two of the estipite *columns fallen from the portal decoration.*
—Courtesy Arizona State Museum.

William Dinwiddie's 1894 view shows damage from the 1887 earthquake; the mortuary and atrium walls have fallen and only three columns remain around the portal. The auxiliary buildings have been expanded and provided with a sloping roof. Papago houses stretch into the distance. —Courtesy Special Collections, University of Arizona Library.

The portal before restoration in 1907. The fragile estipite columns were nothing more than plastered over adobe bricks and several were destroyed by the 1887 earthquake. —Courtesy Arizona Historical Society.

This 1907 view shows the mission in the final stages of its restoration by Bishop Henry Granjon. The atrium wall is being rebuilt and the church has taken on its distinctive white appearance. —Courtesy Arizona Historical Society.

TUMACACORI

J. Ross Browne drew this somewhat exaggerated sketch in 1864.—From Adventures in the Apache Country.

By 1913 the attic above the facade had fallen. It and the roof were restored in the early 1920s.—Photo by Robert H. Forbes, Arizona Historical Society.

SAN IGNACIO

Dinwiddie posed townspeople in his shot of San Ignacio in 1894. A large section of the scalloped cemetery wall was still standing.—Courtesy Smithsonian Institution.

The folk charm of the portal and its carved doors are the hallmark of San Ignacio.—Photo by George A. Grant, 1935, Western Archaeological Center, National Park Service.

In 1925 the interior at San Ignacio appeared much as it does today. The main difference is the presence of the portable side altar on the left.—Photo by George Boundey, Western Archaeological Center.

MAGDALENA

Browne's 1864 sketch shows the present parish church on the left and the church of Father Agustín de Campos on the right.

An unknown photographer made this view ca. 1900 and it confirms the accuracy of Browne's sketch. The espadaña atop the facade had been removed and new trees and walkways better defined the plaza.—Courtesy Southwest Museum, Los Angeles.

By 1934 the church had been totally "secularized" and was converted into a meeting hall for the anti-clerical political party and the national peasant and workers union. Housing a library rounded out its functions.—Photo by Robert H. Rose, Western Archaeological Center.

TUBUTAMA

This view by an unknown photographer ca. 1890 shows a weathered church and barren plaza. Note the two little towers atop the facade, which though charming, overly cluttered the roofline; they were removed soon after. —Courtesy Arizona State Museum.

The crossing and sanctuary in 1935, showing that even the wooden altarpiece had been removed to guard it from anti-clerics. The statues have been hidden away and bird droppings litter the floor and niches. —Photo by Grant, Western Archaeological Center.

OQUITOA

A 1925 photo shows the 19th century retablo a few years before it was taken down. The columns are neoclassic but the style and organization remain baroque. The oil paintings it contained now hang in the sacristy. —Photo by Boundey, Western Archaeological Center.

A stark view in 1935 with the statues hidden away. The previous retablo was dismantled, leaving only the neo-Gothic niche for St. Anthony, and parts of it imaginatively re-used to construct a new altar. —Photo by Grant, Western Archaeological Center.

CABORCA

The main altar in 1894. The elements are neoclassic but they have been so arranged and then decorated with tinsel and paper that the effect remains very much baroque. Note the estipite-like artifical columns flanking the central niche.—Photo by Dinwiddie, Smithsonian Institution.

A staged portrait of the mission in 1895. Note the buildings on the left, now completely disappeared. Photo by Reyes, Western Archaeological Center.

By 1908 flood waters had begun to eat away at the rear of the building; here already destroying most of the convento. Photo by Forbes, Arizona Historical Society.

The flooding continued, eventually destroying the sanctuary and south transcept but the dome miraculously survived. In the 1950s the bank was reinforced in preparation for rebuilding the lost sections.—Courtesy Arizona Historical Society.

THE DISCOVERY OF PADRE KINO'S GRAVE

From time immemorial history has explained the monuments of man's changing achievements. But in modern times man achieves change so rapidly that his links to the past are lost in the pace of change itself. History is no longer enough. So in recent decades man has developed the skill to search the ruins of his past to bring greater meaning to his present. The science of archaeology and the art of history have become as significant as astronautics and bio-physics because they create the perspective of man's cultural and scientific growth.

In this way the tiny town of Magdalena de Kino in Sonora, Mexico, is as significant as Guaymas with its satellite tracking station. Here in Magdalena in May, 1966, a team of anthropologists and historians located and identified the grave of Padre Eusebio Francisco Kino. The successful discovery climaxed nearly forty years of frustrating failures.

When Herbert E. Bolton, as a young historian, published his translation of *Kino's Memoirs of the Pimería Alta* in 1919, he speculated that Padre Kino's remains had been transferred to San Ignacio de Caborica. Or at least that's what the local rumor of the time said. Apparently Bolton and Professor Frank Lockwood probed the foundations of the present church around 1928 to find Kino's grave. That's how the story is told today. But by the time Bolton published his renowned biography of Padre Kino, the *Rim of Christendom*, in 1936, he dropped any mention of Kino's transferral to San Ignacio. The record of Kino's burial in the little chapel of San Francisco Xavier stood as the single, reliable record of history about his grave. But where was that grave? Where was the chapel? Indeed, where was the town in 1711? Unknown to almost everyone was Bolton's own opinion. Writing to Professor Lockwood, he told him he would "walk over the Padre's grave as he approached the church of Santa María Magdalena."

Many Mexican anthropologists and historians tried to discover the obscured grave. Serapio Dávila in 1928 undertook an extensive search. He opened trenches in front of the present church and found the cemented foundations of an old parochial structure. Soon his workers were uncovering hordes of scattered bones, part of an old cemetery. How would one ever tell Kino's grave from any other? Dávila gave up.

Through the decades of the 30's and the 40's Professor Eduardo W. Villa, Rubén Parodi, Professor Fernando Pesqueira, and Señorita Dolores Encinas devoted their talents to solve the mystery of the missing site. But each effort ended in failure. New theories and newer rumors arose to explain the failures, thus creating only more confusion. In 1961 *Arizona Highways* dedicated their March issue to Padre Eusebio Kino — 250 years after his death in Magdalena. The state of Arizona was justly proud of its pioneer padre but the circumstances of the dedication rekindled the same perplexing question: where was Kino's grave? In a gesture toward solution Editor Raymond Carlson incorporated into the issue an article by Donald Page in collaboration with Colonel Gilbert Proctor. The article focused attention on a complex of private dwellings on Calle Pesqueira some four blocks distant from the present church. Oldtimers called the place, "La Capilla." Indeed the structure looked like a chapel with its arches, niches, and scalloped passageways. Beyond what he had written Donald Page could not be consulted about his reasons for thinking this was the chapel of San Francisco Xavier; Page was dead. Colonel Proctor remained firmly convinced this was the authentic burial chapel.

Former failures to find the grave and new rumors reinforced each other until the residents of Magdalena could sit idle no longer. The grave should be found. In the late spring of 1963 the Magdalena Lions Club obtained the permission of the Villa family to excavate the rooms of their family home on Calle Pesqueira. Curiously, the searchers found a subterranean tile floor, broken through in three places as if a coffin and two boxes had been removed through it. The rubble from the hole contained an old shoe, some beer bottles, and a cigarette lighter, indicating it had probably been refilled in the late 1920's. Many

The capilla of San Francisco Xavier and the mission of Padre Agustín de Campos in Magdalena, Sonora, as conceived by Dr. Jorge Olvera. View from the present church.

interpreted this discovery as evidence for the removal of Kino's remains (for protective custody) during the religious persecution of President Calles' regime.

A slow, careful investigation was then begun in the summer of 1963 by the Reverend Charles Polzer, S.J., to evaluate the findings of the Lions Club project and to sort rumor from fact. With the help of Dr. William Wasley, resident archaeologist of the Arizona State Museum, it became evident that the excavation of "Proctor's Chapel," as *La Capilla* came to be known, were inconclusive *at best*. In fact everything pointed to this site's being wholly incorrect. If true, then Kino had never been there to be removed!

Further historical investigations were undertaken in 1964 by Father Polzer. They were conclusive: the Proctor site was false. An archaeological survey of other Kino mission sites in the Pimería further corroborated Polzer and Wasley's objections to the validity of the Proctor site. But the discovery of the unusual openings in the tile floor of the "chapel" convinced the people that Padre Kino's bones had been carried off to safety decades ago. Rumor persisted and Magdalena was a maze of conflicting opinion.

While preparations for the Kino Memorial Statue neared completion, the search for Kino's grave was shelved. In February, 1965, the nation was introduced to the prominence of Padre Kino by the unveiling of his statue in the nation's Capitol. Little did the people responsible for the statue realize what they had wrought for the discovery of Kino's grave. Mexico, too, was justly proud of Padre Kino; the Mexican people were not about to forfeit their share in Kino's fame.

Hence, at the request of Mexican President Díaz Ordaz, the Secretary of Public Education, Agustín Yáñez, commissioned Professor Wigberto Jiménez Moreno, the director of the Department of Historical Investigation of the National Institute of Anthropology and History, to find the remains of Padre Kino. It was June 30, 1965. Whatever legal log-jams the Americans conjectured over in the search for Kino's grave were swept away by the executive order of the Mexican federal government. Professor Jiménez Moreno, Dr. Jorge Olvera, the colonial art historian, and Professor Arturo Romano, the physical anthropologist of the National Institute, began a systematic search of the archives for information about the grave.

59

A quick trip to the Sonora frontier in August, 1965, acquainted Jiménez Moreno and Olvera with their newly inherited problem. Rumors and opinions varied on all aspects: the grave, the chapel, the remains, and their transfer. Professor Jiménez Moreno retired to Mexico City profoundly aware he had more on his hands than a casual search. Dr. Olvera remained behind to begin the methodic excavations which eventually crisscrossed the site of the ancient pueblo.

The traditional Fiesta of San Francisco forced an interruption of work in October. The trenches were backfilled and the investigators took advantage of the recess to evaluate their problem. Professor Jiménez Moreno accurately reassessed the situation. The discovery of the grave and the verification of the remains of Padre Kino would be no simple matter. The ingredients of success would be men and knowledge, both archaeological and historical.

It was April, 1966, when the team arrived again in Magdalena. Jiménez Moreno invited other qualified investigators to join the team. Padre Cruz Acuña from Hermosillo pitched in to comb through old diocesan archives and to interview oldtimers. The Reverend Kieran McCarty, O.F.M., historian of San Xavier del Bac (Tucson), signed on as research historian; his familiarity with Franciscan records aided materially in piecing out the fate of the old chapel. Dr. William Wasley was placed on detached service from the Arizona State Museum; his keen knowledge of the archaeology of the area provided the team with essential knowledge and skills. The chemist from the local clinic, Dr. Gabriel Sánchez de la Vega, gave invaluable service as the man most acquainted with the recent attempts to find the grave.

To the men of Mexico City in 1965 the search for the grave of Padre Kino appeared to be a simple matter. To the same men on the scene in Magdalena in 1966 the search was recognized as enormously complicated, and perhaps impossible. Excitement charged the air of Magdalena as the experts challenged the unknown.

Professor Jiménez Moreno understood his problem well. Here was a situation that required solution by a process of elimination. Units of the team spread out from Magdalena to probe each site favored by certain rumors and opinions. No reasonable possibility was overlooked, but one by one they were being eliminated as archaeological and historical evidence piled up.

Slowly the circle of probability narrowed to the plaza in front of the Magdalena church. Over two kilometers of exploratory trenches wandered through the town. Work crews exposed foundations of buildings long since forgotten. The earth yielded the bones of countless human beings.

It seemed as though the search would succumb to the intricacies of its own method. Then the breaks began to come. The historians were building up key clues about the chapel from the archives. The major find was a description of the little chapel of San Francisco Xavier in an 1828 report by don Fernando Grande:

The chapel of this town is moderate. It is of adobe material. The entrance faces south. There is a moderate little tower in which are located three bells and another small one. It has nothing particular that draws attention. The principal and only altar is in the chancel. On it are set an image of the crucified Christ and another of the Virgin of Dolores; at the feet of the larger carving is the littler one of ordinary quality. And in some niches which form a reredos along the wall of the altar are set the statue of St. Magdalene, the patron of the pueblo (it's small but well carved), one of St. Francis Xavier and one of Blessed Joseph Oriol; the latter are imperfectly carved. Midway in the nave of the church is a niche where there is located in a case a large carving of St. Francis Xavier, an object of devotion everywhere in the northwest. It is a beautiful and serious sculpture . . .

The team that discovered Kino's grave:
left to right; P. Santos Saenz, W. W. Wasley, Jiménez Moreno, J. Olvera, José Matiella, and E. Burrus, S. J. (members not shown; Rev. K. McCarty, O.F.M., A. Romano, and G. Sánchez de la Vega).

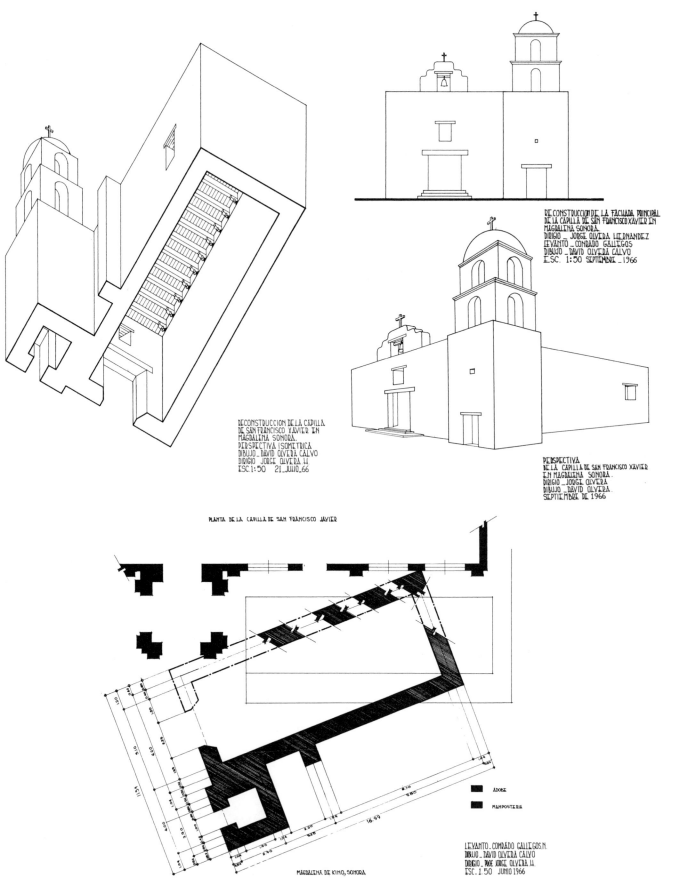

RECONSTRUCCION DE LA FACHADA PRINCIPAL
DE LA CAPILLA DE SAN FRANCISCO XAVIER IN
MAGDALENA SONORA.
DIRIGIO _ JORGE OLVERA HERNANDEZ
LEVANTO _ CONRADO GALLEGOS
DIBUJO _ DAVID OLVERA CALVO
ESC. 1:50 SEPTIEMBRE _ 1966

RECONSTRUCCION DE LA CAPILLA
DE SAN FRANCISCO XAVIER IN
MAGDALENA SONORA.
PERSPECTIVA ISOMETRICA
DIBUJO _ DAVID OLVERA CALVO
DIRIGIO _ JORGE OLVERA H.
ESC. 1:50 21_JULIO_66

PERSPECTIVA
DE LA CAPILLA DE SAN FRANCISCO XAVIER
IN MAGDALENA SONORA.
DIRIGIO _ JORGE OLVERA.
DIBUJO _ DAVID OLVERA.
SEPTIEMBRE DE 1966

PLANTA DE LA CAPILLA DE SAN FRANCISCO JAVIER

ADOBE

MAMPOSTERIA

LEVANTO_CONRADO GALLEGOS M.
DIBUJO _ DAVID OLVERA CALVO
DIRIGIO _ PROF JORGE OLVERA H.
ESC. 1:50 JUNIO 1966

MAGDALENA DE KINO, SONORA.

The facade, perspective, and isometric projection of the capilla of San Francisco Xavier in Magdalena, Sonora; the reconstruction was composed by Professor Olvera and drawn by David Olvera.

61

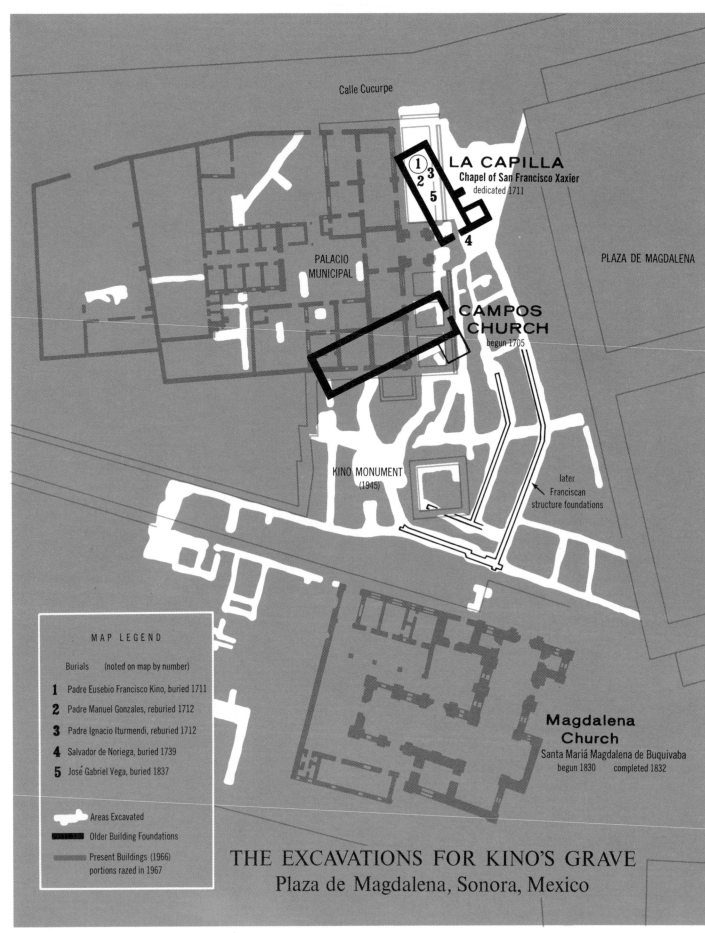

Calle Cucurpe

① 1 3
2 3
5

LA CAPILLA
Chapel of San Francisco Xaxier
dedicated 1711

4

PALACIO
MUNICIPAL

PLAZA DE MAGDALENA

CAMPOS
CHURCH
begun 1705

KINO MONUMENT
(1945)

later
Franciscan
structure foundations

MAP LEGEND

Burials   (noted on map by number)

1 Padre Eusebio Francisco Kino, buried 1711

2 Padre Manuel Gonzales, reburied 1712

3 Padre Ignacio Iturmendi, reburied 1712

4 Salvador de Noriega, buried 1739

5 José Gabriel Vega, buried 1837

Areas Excavated

Older Building Foundations

Present Buildings (1966)
portions razed in 1967

Magdalena
Church
Santa Mariá Magdalena de Buquivaba
begun 1830   completed 1832

THE EXCAVATIONS FOR KINO'S GRAVE
Plaza de Magdalena, Sonora, Mexico

The remains of Padre Kino in Magdalena, Sonora.

From the burial register two more relevant facts were learned. In 1739 a Spaniard, Salvador de Noriega, was buried at the entrance to the chapel. Nearly a century later a ninety year old Indian resident, José Gabriel Vega, was buried before the niche of St. Francis Xavier.

While the historians read through miles of microfilm and dusted off old records, the archaeological teams followed the clues exposed by their trenching. The cement foundations in front of the church which had occupied Dávila years before were soon discounted when it was learned that lime was not used for construction in the Pimería during the earlier Jesuit period. Traces of adobe walls became more evident as the work crews learned the difficult art of distinguishing an adobe foundation from the alluvial deposits natural to the terrain. One wall which ran east and west had attracted the attention of Dr. Olvera who felt that it maintained the proper orientation shown in some mid-nineteenth century sketches of the pueblo. But what is one wall in the middle of a whole town?

Dr. Wasley convinced the team of the need to correlate their findings with known Jesuit ruins in the Pimería. And on the very day Wasley, Olvera, and Romano were making their reconnaissance, the workmen in the trench that followed Olvera's favored wall came to its end. Professor Jiménez saw that they had really reached a corner. The wall turned toward the City Hall. This was the first clear indication that it might define the foundations of a building.

Earlier in the exploration a crew had followed a lateral trench from Olvera's wall. Close to the north-south axis of the main trench they exposed a skeleton which Professor Romano identified as that of a European. Everyone regarded the discovery as "Suspect Number One." But then the pieces of the puzzle began to fall into place. "Suspect Number One" was on the south side of the adobe wall, and now that the long adobe wall to the east of the burial had turned a corner westward, there was little doubt that the Number One Suspect was Salvador de Noriega.

The east wall of the building showed the evidence of a small buttress about midway. This corresponded to another historical discovery that Padre José Pérez Llera in 1828 erected a buttress to prevent the wall from further slumping! The corner discovered on the day the team was reconnoitering other missions proved to be that of the apse of the chapel. Cautiously the crews followed the line of the adobe and boulder foundation. The sharp spades cut through the soil ever so carefully. A shovelful of earth spewed into the screen. Nothing. Then at the base of the trench fell a piece of a skull, dislodged from the edge! A cry! Tension mounted as Dr. Wasley, Dr. Olvera, Dr. Romano and Professor Jiménez Moreno carefully exposed the whole skull. Could it be? Could it really be Kino's? It was 4:45 on the afternoon of May 19, 1966.

The entire team concentrated on the complex of trenches that seemed now to be located on the site of the ancient chapel. The skeleton discovered that fateful afternoon was delicately uncovered. The earth within the entire chapel area was cautiously peeled back. Then the key elements began to fall in place without complication. "Kino" was an original burial on the Gospel side of the chapel; the body had rested between the second and third foundation support, just as the burial record of Padre Agustín de Campos said. Then at Kino's feet but closer to the west wall appeared a "secondary burial," one that had

Enlarged detail of the crucifix found in the grave.

been transferred from another place. Across the chapel floor area, on the Epistle side of the apse, another secondary burial was uncovered in the packed earth. Fantastic! but predictable if this were really the chapel. In 1712, one year after Kino's burial in the chapel, Padre Campos transferred the bodies of Padres Iturmendi and González from Tubutama and interred them in the same chapel on the Epistle and the Gospel side respectively.

Midway down the body of the church the excavators came upon another burial of a very old Indian man. Another key slipped into place because 90 year old José Gabriel Vega was buried before the niche of St. Francis Xavier — located half way down the nave! And Salvador de Noriega was still lying patiently at the southerly entrance.

Professor Romano carefully studied the skeleton which lay on the gospel side of the building — if this were really the chapel. The man had been in his 60's. Kino had been 66. The skull was a classic European type from the Alpine region. Kino was from the Tyrol. The tibia bones of the legs showed a pronounced retroflexion. This was characteristic of the mountain people of Kino's homeland. When Wasley and Olvera

removed the last traces of the wooden coffin which had caved in on the chest of the skeleton, they found a small bronze cross lying on the clavicle. This was typical of the Jesuit missionary of the seventeenth century.

On May 21, 1966, the team reached the conclusion that it had in fact discovered the long lost remains of Padre Eusebio Francisco Kino. On May 24 the announcement was made to the general public; no doubt remained in the minds of any of the team or the experts called in after the initial conclusion was reached. The Reverend Ernest Burrus of the Jesuit Historical Institute at Rome agreed in full. And finally on July 14, 1966, the Academy of History met in Mexico City to review the evidence. Professor Jiménez Moreno presented seventy-two depositions explaining the discovery. Then, Dr. Alberto Caso in the name of the Mexican Academy of History pronounced in favor of the identity of the remains. Padre Kino was found at last.

As with everything that man does, there are always those who doubt. Some wanted the archaeologists to uncover a plaque or headstone. None ever existed, particularly for a man like Kino. He died as he had lived, in poverty and in the presence of his Lord. What the doubters had forgotten was that the monument over his grave was not just a headstone, but a chapel, and not just a cross with a name, but a whole culture.

So conclusive is the evidence which the team under Professor Jiménez Moreno uncovered that if the skeleton had been marked with another name, the anthropologists and historians would have realized someone was trying to play a joke.

But perhaps the most remarkable thing of all is that when the anthropologists were asked to reconstruct the likeness of Kino from his skeletal remains, they shrugged and pointed to a sketch on the wall of the City Hall. There hung the drawing done by Mrs. Frances O'Brien of Tucson. One could hardly come any closer to the human reality. She had sketched his portrait from the salient features of the Chini family as they lived in this century. She had only hoped to approximate Kino's likeness. Little did she know she had drawn the last clue in the recognition of Padre Eusebio Kino.

THE PADRE KINO MEMORIAL PLAZA

The discovery of Padre Kino's grave in 1966 only set the stage for change in Magdalena. Hardly had the discovery team completed its work before Professor Wigberto Jiménez Moreno suggested that the town be officially renamed "Magdalena de Kino" in the Mexican fashion of commemorating her heros. Kino's remains could not be left unprotected from the weather or unguarded from the curious and devout. Jiménez Moreno also urged some suitable memorial be designed.

The tiny population of Magdalena had inherited a whole new set of problems that were going to require cooperative efforts to solve. Scientific technicians from the University of Arizona's department of anthropology were invited to treat Kino's bones with special preservatives. The soil underneath was impregnated with plasticizers to stabilize the grave site. Covered by a metal roofed shed, a sealed glass vault encased the remains that were left *in situ*.

Patiently the mayor at the time, Gerardo Nava, looked from his office door on the final resting place of Kino. Streams of visitors passed beside the excavations and impeded the efficiency of operations at the city hall. What were the city fathers to do with the grave of a promi-

nent hero at their doorstep? Nava smiled and opened negotiations to move all of the city hall to the old Palacio Municipal, three blocks away.

So it was that Magdalena waited while federal, state and local officials pondered the proper solution. The care of the grave site passed on to the *Instituto Nacional de Antropología e Historia,* who designated Gabriel Sánchez de la Vega as chief custodian. Meanwhile the architect Medillín visited Magdalena and devised some initial plans for a monument. The Governor of Sonora, Lic. Luis Encinas, appointed a six man committee of Magdalena citizens to oversee the acquisition of property for the planned monument and to direct the demolition of buildings. Magdalena was on the move.

Then a group of prominent Magdalena citizens, who also served on the Comité del Monumento del Padre Kino, appealed to the Mexican federal government for a change in plans in the development of the Kino monument. Acquiescing to their desires, the government referred the project to the new Governor of Sonora, Faustino Félix Serna. He initiated a completely new plan — more comprehensive, more ambitious, and more in accord with the local situation. Subsequently, the architect Francisco Artigas, who

distinguished himself in the colonial restorations of Guanajuato, was invited to design the Plaza of Padre Kino in Magdalena.

Artigas' problem consisted in the integration of several architectural features. The grave was not to be touched; the church was to be remodeled; and a site for a museum and library were to be included. His solution focused each element on a sunken octagonal fountain, thus achieving integration with simplicity and balance. The entire fifteen acre plaza was enclosed by *portales* (arched, beamed walkways) reminiscent of eighteenth century building design.

While the details of construction were being worked out, the Comité in Magdalena began the difficult task of relocating the many families who lived in the affected area. Homes the inhabitants

considered ancestral were to be levelled for the plaza. With an admirable sense of civic pride, and not without sacrifice, these families moved into newer houses provided in other parts of town. Over 7,000 square yards of buildings were removed to prepare for new construction.

Who paid the bill? Everyone seems to ask. The citizens of Magdalena, individually and through civic groups, contributed over one million pesos toward the ten million pesos project. The rest of the financing came through matched donations from the federal and state governments. Cooperation was the key to the Plaza's creation.

In January of 1970 the *Constructora Federal de Escuelas Públicas* (CAFPCE) began work under the direction of the engineer Francisco Fernández. The restoration of the church was given over to the engineer Juan José Lecanda. Using local materials and labor, architect Gustavo Aguilar from Hermosillo pressed completion of the entire complex by December of the same year.

Before the Plaza was begun the future president of Mexico, Lic. Luis Echeverría Alvarez, visited Magdalena in December, 1969. Expressing his admiration for the gigantic labors of Padre Kino in advancing civilization in northwestern Mexico, he solemnly promised to return to inaugurate the memorial plaza. He kept his promise on May 2, 1971; a finished plaza and a proud population awaited him. At noon that day the newly elected President of Mexico visited the crypt while rolls of applause came from the "Pimalteños" who knew their President shared the enthusiasm of their heritage.

Magdalena de Kino now guards the mortal remains of the Padre on Horseback. More splendor than Kino ever knew on the desert trails of the Pimería Alta surrounds him in the Plaza that bears his name. He was a man who enjoyed good art and good architecture. He was proud of the churches the Indians had built at Dolores, Remedios and Cocóspera. And he thrilled at the sight of hundreds of his friends coming across the deserts to share in celebrations. How does he feel now, centuries later, when thousands come to visit this latest monument erected in his honor?

THE STATUES OF PADRE KINO

Statues are made of storied men, but seldom are stories written about statues. This, however, is the story of a statue; in fact, two statues. The man who first considered Kino an apt subject for monumental art was Father Manuel González, then rector of the mission at Oposura. When Kino was conceiving his great expedition to the Colorado in 1700 to prove that California was not an island, Father González wrote him: "If you accomplish this, we must erect to you a costly and famous statue. And if the way is short there will be two statues." The way to California was not short, but the accomplishments of Kino's career have merited him two statues anyway.

The state of Arizona decided to honor Father Eusebio Francisco Kino in 1961 when several Arizona legislators introduced a Joint Memorial (No. 5) asking that the Congress of the United States accept Padre Kino as the subject for the state's second statue in the national Hall of Statuary. Padre Kino had by that time already been recognized as the state's first pioneer, explorer, and cartographer.

The statue proposal and resolution created new problems because the regulations for statues in the National Hall will not permit purely imaginary conceptions of historical persons. Since no known portrait of Kino existed, the unusual procedure of making a composite portrait from photos of family descendants, using salient and recurrent features, was devised. A special committee designated by Governor Paul Fannin then commissioned the renowned Tucson artist Frances O'Brien to portray Kino as he may have looked.

Once the portrait was submitted and accepted by the special Kino Memorial Statue Committee all the other pertinent facts about Kino and the dress of his times were compiled into a brochure which was distributed to all sculptors who cared to enter the competition arranged by the statue commission.

From a field of twenty-six entries the committee narrowed the competition to two finalists: George Phippen and Madame Suzanne Silvercruys. Both statues displayed exemplary skill, but the rendering of Padre Kino by Baroness Silvercruys retained more elements of the historical personage and the committee decided in her favor.

The half-size model was shipped to Connecticut where Madame Silvercruys began the complex task of fashioning a seven-foot version of Kino for the National Hall of Statuary. Molten copper from Arizona mines flowed into the precision cast and Father Kino emerged to take his place among the great founders of this nation.

On February 14, 1965, the first statue of Father Kino was unveiled before a crowd of seven hundred people from all over the nation and the world. The dedication ceremony took place on the same spot where the body of President John F. Kennedy, who had signed the bill admitting Father Kino into the National Hall, had lain in state. It had taken two hundred and sixty-five years, but Father Kino was honored in the way Father González had predicted so long ago.

Father Ernest Burrus, S.J., from the Jesuit Historical Institute in Rome, summarized the significance of Kino in his dedicatory address:

> We can feel justified in dedicating this statue not merely to the memory of one man, however great he may be; we dedicate it to all Americans who would share Kino's high ideals, lofty aspirations, and his bold vision of the future to bring together all peoples in true understanding and in an abiding communion of spirit; we dedicate this statue to the citizens, present and future, of Arizona whose pioneer founder he was; we dedicate it to our neighbors of Mexico, especially to those of Sonora who have preserved his memory in such deep affection; we dedicate it to Kino's native land and to the people and region from which he came; we dedicate it to the peoples of the lands of his adoption, whether in Austria, Bavaria, or Spain, where Kino spent so many of his intensely active years; finally we dedicate this statue of Father Eusebio Francisco Kino to all peoples and to all nations of good will and of high ideals.

These final, ringing words of praise, dedicating the statue, were not final at all. The Mexican delegation realized that Father Kino was more than an Arizona pioneer; he was a symbol even centuries later of the friendship between nations and the dreams of future prosperity. In a matter of weeks the President of Mexico, Gustavo Díaz

Equestrian statue by Julián Martínez

Ordaz, ordered the grave of Father Kino to be located so that a fitting memorial could be erected to this giant of the Americas.

The tale of discovery constitutes one of those marvels of modern history and archaeological science. Even though no portrait of Kino is extant today the discovery of his remains in Magdalena has enabled scientists, employing techniques of physical anthropology, and artists to reconstruct his likeness with amazing accuracy.

Realizing the importance of Father Kino to the Mexican-American frontier, Governor Luis Encinas Johnson of Sonora commissioned a famed sculptor in Mexico City to depict Kino on horseback. Don Julián Martínez made a careful study of the skeleton of Kino discovered in Magdalena and formed a powerful figure in bronze to match the man who conquered the desert trails. Two statues were cast and the first was erected in Hermosillo, the capital of Sonora. It stands at the northern entrance to the city, dominating the panoramic landscape of the San Miguel and Sonora river valley.

The second statue was presented by Governor Encinas to the Governor and people of Arizona. The spectacular bronze statue was dedicated on the lawn of the capitol in Phoenix in an impressive all Spanish program.

Now the statue of Father Kino stands in each capital as a symbol of a common heritage from the man whose dedicated life brought civilization and hope to a previously unknown frontier.

The Arizona dedication ceremonies included a unique look backward and forward in time. By placing a "time capsule" in the base of the statue Arizonans reviewed their land as it was known to Father Kino, as it is known today, and as they predict it to be 272 years from now. It was 272 years before the dedication that Father Kino first set foot in Arizona.

With the dedication of the second statue the prediction of Father Manuel González was fulfilled. And there is every reason to suspect that southwestern artists will not cease to reinterpret the Padre on Horseback in painting and sculpture. The unique talent of Ted deGrazia has already been trained on Father Kino in an extensive series of paintings prepared for the two hundred and fiftieth anniversary of Kino's death. One can well understand why Father Kino is the subject of art because he embodies an authentic western spirit that encompasses virility, vision, and an awesome sense of peace and purpose.

Plastelina model by Suzanne Silvercruys

A READING GUIDE TO THE MISSIONS

BANNON, JOHN FRANCIS, S. J. *The Spanish Borderlands Frontier 1513–1821*. New York: Holt, Rinehart and Winston, 1970; 308 pp. Best historical synthesis to date.

BOLTON, HERBERT E. *Padre on Horseback*. San Francisco: Sonora Press, 1932. Reprint, Chicago: Loyola University Press, 1963; introduction by John F. Bannon, S. J.

———. *The Rim of Christendom*. New York: Macmillan, 1936. Reprint, New York: Russell and Russell, 1960. This is the definitive biography of Eusebio Francisco Kino.

BURRUS, ERNEST J., S. J. *Kino and Manje, Explorers of Sonora and Arizona*. Rome and St. Louis: Jesuit Historical Institute, 1971.

———. *Kino and the Cartography of Northwestern New Spain*. Tucson: Arizona Pioneer's Historical Society, 1965.

CLARK, ANN NOLAN. *Father Kino, Priest to the Pimas*. New York: Farrar, Straus, 1963. For children 7–12 years.

DONOHUE, JOHN AUGUSTINE, S. J. *After Kino: Jesuit Missions in Northwestern New Spain, 1711–1767*. Rome and St. Louis: Jesuit Historical Institute, 1969.

ECKHART, GEORGE B. and James S. Griffith. *Temples in the Wilderness: Spanish Churches of Northern Sonora*. Tucson: Arizona Historical Society, Historical Monograph #3. 104pp. Brief histories and descriptions of the major churches in the mission chain.

KESSELL, JOHN L. *Mission of Sorrows: Jesuit Guevavi and the Pimas*. Tucson: The University of Arizona Press, 1970.

———. *Friars, Soldiers and Reformers: Hispanic Arizona and the Sonoran Mission Frontier, 1767–1858*. Tucson: The University of Arizona Press, 1976. 347pp. The Franciscan Pimería Alta as seen from the vantage point of the Tumacácori mission.

KINO, EUSEBIO FRANCISCO, S. J. *Historical Memoir of the Pimería Alta*. Herbert Bolton, trans. Cleveland: Arthur Clark Co., 1919. 2 vols. Reprint: Berkeley: University of California, 1948. 2 vols. in one.

———. *Kino's Biography of Francisco Javier Saeta*. Translated and with an Epilogue by Charles W. Polzer, S. J.; original Spanish text edited by Ernest J. Burrus, S. J.

———. *Kino's Plan for Development of the Pimería Alta*. Ernest Burrus, S. J., trans. Tucson: Arizona Pioneer's Historical Society, 1961.

———. *Kino Reports to Headquarters*. Ernest Burrus, S. J., trans. Rome: Institutum Historicum Societatis Jesu, 1954.

———. *Kino Writes to the Duchess*. Ernest Burrus, S. J. trans. Rome: Institutum Historicum Societatis Jesu, 1965.

LOCKWOOD, FRANK C. *With Padre Kino on the Trail*. Tucson: The University of Arizona, 1934. Social Science Bulletin No. 5.

MANJE, JUAN MATEO. *Luz de Tierra Incognita: Unknown Arizona and Sonora, 1693–1701*. Translated by Harry J. Karns. Tucson: Arizona Silouettes, 1954. 303pp. The diaries of Kino's trail companion.

NENTWIG, JUAN. *Rudo Ensayo: A Description of Sonora and Arizona in 1764*. Tucson: The University of Arizona Press, 1980. 160 pp. Translated by Albert F. Pradeau and Robert R. Rasmussen. A good historical overview; caution is urged in the botanical section.

PFEFFERKORN, IGNAZ. *Sonora: A Description of the Province*. Translated by Theodore E. Treutlein. Albuquerque: University of New Mexico Press, 1949. 329 pp. A classic contemporary account.

POLZER, CHARLES W., S. J. *Rules and Precepts of the Jesuit Missions of Northwestern New Spain*. Tucson: The University of Arizona Press, 1976. 141 pp.

ROCA, PAUL M. *Paths of the Padres Through Sonora*. Tucson: Arizona Historical Society, 1967. A travelog history of most Sonoran mission sites; historical accounts require critical study.

SMITH, FAY JACKSON, John Kessell, and Francis Fox, S. J. *Father Kino in Arizona*. Phoenix: Arizona Historical Foundation, 1966. This book contains a more complete bibliography on Kino.

SPICER, EDWARD H. *Cycles of Conquest: The Impact of Spain, Mexico and the United States on the Indians of the Southwest, 1533–1960*. Tucson: The University of Arizona Press, 1962. 610 pp.

STEFFAN, JACK. *Kino and the Trail to the Pacific*. New York: P. J. Kenedy, 1960. For younger readers.

THAYER, JOHN. *Desert Padre, Eusebio Francisco Kino*. Milwaukee: Bruce, 1959. Another book for the young reader.

WYLLYS, RUFUS KAY. *Pioneer Padre; the Life and Times of Eusebio Francisco Kino*. Dallas: Southwest Press, 1935.

ACUÑA GALVEZ, P. CRUZ. *El Romance del Padre Kino*. México: Editorial Jus, 1970; Colección México Heroico Núm. 104.

TRUEBA, ALFONSO. *El Padre Kino: Misionero Itinerante y Ecuestre*. México: Editorial Jus, 1960; Figuras y Episodios Núm. 23.

ABOUT THE AUTHOR

Charles W. Polzer, S. J., has been actively researching and writing about Father Kino since his coming to Arizona in 1958. He is a member of the California Province of the Society of Jesus which he entered in 1952 after receiving his baccalaureate from the University of Santa Clara. He pursued graduate studies in philosophy, theology and government at St. Louis University and Santa Clara University for which he was awarded Masters degrees and a Licentiate in Philosophy. In 1972 he completed the requirements for the Doctorate in Philosophy in History and Anthropology at the University of Arizona. Throughout this time he continued to write and lecture in historical subjects dealing with the greater Southwest.

Father Polzer is a native of San Diego, California, where he first became interested in the history of the Southwest. After serving for three years as an instructor at Brophy College Preparatory in Phoenix, Arizona, he continued to dedicate himself to a broad spectrum of Southwestern studies. He was instrumental in founding the Southwestern Mission Research Center which was affiliated for several years with the Arizona Historical Society and is now based at the Arizona State Museum.

Since 1974 Father Polzer has held the position of Ethnohistorian at the Arizona State Museum of the University of Arizona. In that capacity he has directed a program of basic research and publication entitled the Documentary Relations of the Southwest. This program is responsible for the design and creation of an extended, computerized data base of primary documents on northern New Spain. Documentary histories have been prepared using this data base as the principal means of selection and annotation. These innovative methods have opened entire new areas of research and analysis in social history for the greater Southwest.

ABOUT THE CARTOGRAPHER

Donald Bufkin has been primarily responsible for the cartography and design layout for the *Kino Guide II*. He is also a native Californian who came to Arizona's Sonoran desert nearly a quarter century ago. His early education brought him to Pasadena City College and the Art Center School in Los Angeles. By profession he became a city planner and rose to the directorship of the Pima Association of Government Transportation Planning Agency. He relinquished that position in 1975 to become the Associate Director of the Arizona Historical Society, a role for which he was well prepared by his long association with Western studies. He has been a major contributor to many articles and studies in Western history because of his distinguished ability as

a cartographer and his keen knowledge of historical data.

FOOTNOTES AND ACKNOWLEDGEMENTS

The text of *Kino Guide II* has purposely omitted all scholarly apparatus in order to present the reader with an uninterrupted and unemcumbered account. For the sake of those whose interest in Father Eusebio Kino and the missions of the Pimería may have been enkindled by this brief volume, the reader is referred to the still definitive biography of Father Kino by Dr. Herbert Eugene Bolton, *The Rim of Christendom*. The bibliography of works on Father Kino is so extensive that it precludes publication in a work of this nature. however, the reader may be assured that the contents have been developed from the majority of known works on Father Kino, original manuscript material, correspondence, and critical appraisals.

The section on the history of the Pimería before Father Kino and the Jesuit period after him depends on the author's own published works and original research. The section on Franciscan history has been developed from the excellent research and publications of Rev. Kieran McCarty, OFM, and Dr. John Kessell, some of whose works appear in the Reading Guide.

The selection and analysis of historic photography was done by Thomas H. Naylor who has spent more than a decade on Spanish colonial research, especially in field situations. His expertise in dendrochonology has brought him to hundreds of colonial sites throughout Mexico.

PHOTOGRAPHIC AND ART CREDITS

All photographs in *Kino Guide II* were taken by the author except in the following instances:

COVER: Sketch of Padre Kino by Frances O'Brien, Tucson. Courtesy of the Arizona Historical Society, Tucson.

TITLE PAGE: Artistic rendering of the seal of the Province of New Spain of the Society of Jesus (1700) by Cal Cook, Tucson.

INTRODUCTION: Golden Gate Peak, Tucson. Edward Ronstadt.

Page 6: Pima Indian. Bureau of American Ethology.

Page 12: Casa Grande. Arizona Historical Society, Tucson.

Page 22: San Miguel de Oposura (Moctezuma). George B. Eckhart Collection.

Page 46: Tumacácori, NE view. W. Cline Company, Chattanooga, Tenn.

Page 49: San Xavier del Bac, interior. Helga Teiwes, Arizona State Museum.

Page 51–57: Credits noted on each caption in this section.

Page 59: Original sketch by Jorge Olvera, Mexico City.

Page 61: Original perspectives by Jorge and David Olvera, Mexico City.

Page 63: Fr. Polzer and Padre Kino. Edward Ronstadt, Tucson.

Page 64: Detail of Kino's crucifix. Jorge Olvera, Mexico City.

Page 65: Magdalena excavations 1966. Jorge Olvera, Mexico City.

Page 70: Kino Statue, Washington, D. C. Yousef Karsh, Ottawa, Canada.

Page 72: Kino on horseback. Jorge Olvera, Mexico City.

Page 74: Author, Charles Polzer, S. J.; Thomas C. Barnes, Tucson. Cartographer, Don Bufkin: Thomas H. Naylor, Tucson.

SOUTHWESTERN MISSION RESEARCH CENTER

The Southwestern Mission Research Center (SMRC) was incorporated in 1965 by several scholars and others interested in the colonial history and anthropology of the greater Southwest. Historians and anthropologists have long recognized that mission records from this epoch continue to provide the single, richest source of available information. Hence the research center attributed to itself the name "Southwestern Mission," but none of its interests or functions are "missionary" in the ordinary sense of that term today. The SMRC has no ecclesiastical connection except indirectly through its members.

Although many knowledgeable persons have probed into the fascinating and relatively unknown history of northern New Spain for over a half century, vast amounts of study still await future scholars and writers. The complex and challenging saga of native American cultures, European contact, and social interaction remains to be understood and described. The task is so enormous that no individual or group effort has matched it. By creating the SMRC its founders only hoped to address a part of the problem by providing institutional continuity, shared knowledge, and intellectual resiliency. Whether those goals will have been achieved can only be proven by the achievements of the SMRC membership.

The SMRC has begun to serve as a much needed clearing-house of information for those engaged in or contemplating research in northern New Spain. For over fifteen years it has published the *SMRC Newsletter* that includes news-notes on current research, research needs, and a pertinent, contemporary bibliography. With a very modest publication fund it has supported the publication of popular monographs on Spanish colonial topics. Its membership now comprises the greater percentage of anthropologists, archaeologists, preservationists, and historians who are actively engaged in southwestern colonial research. Through mutual cooperation and contribution the SMRC attempts to provide the continuity and stability, combined with interdisciplinary variability, that has been lacking in the systematic development of southwestern studies. By supporting research and encouraging publication the SMRC hopes to achieve its goal of recognition for the colonial heritage of the greater Southwest—a recognition much deserved and long overdue.

Incorporated and operated strictly as a non-profit, educational corporation in the State of Arizona, the SMRC is open for membership to anyone genuinely interested in its goals. Annual dues and contributions sutain its research and publication programs; unendowed, its officers and members contribute their efforts for the accomplishment of mutual projects. If you wish to contact the SMRC for any reason, write or call:

Southwestern Mission Research Center,
Arizona State Museum, University of Arizona,
Tucson, Arizona 85721.